UPDATED EXPANDED EDITION

SELF-STUDY

BIBLE
COURSE

ABOUT THE SPIRIT-LED BIBLE STUDY SERIES

The Spirit-Led Bible Study Series is a collection of diverse, stand-alone Bible studies designed for either individuals or groups. Each self-study course features either a scriptural theme or a particular book of the Bible. Readers can go beyond just reading the Bible to become engaged in its truths and principles, learning to apply them to everyday life in practical ways while growing in their understanding of God and deepening their relationship with Him. Jesus said, *"When He, the Spirit of truth, has come, He will guide you into all truth"* (John 16:13). Readers are encouraged to recognize that it is only through the indwelling Holy Spirit that we may truly understand the Scriptures and exhibit the life of Christ in our lives, and that we must intentionally rely on the Spirit in all our reading and study of the Bible.

UPDATED EXPANDED EDITION

SELF-STUDY

BIBLE
COURSE

DEREK PRINCE

WHITAKER
HOUSE

Unless otherwise indicated, all Scripture quotations are taken from the *New King James Version*, © 1979, 1980, 1982, 1984 by Thomas Nelson, Inc. Used by permission. All rights reserved. Scripture quotations marked (NASB) are taken from the updated *New American Standard Bible®*, NASB®, © 1960, 1962, 1963, 1968, 1971, 1972, 1973, 1975, 1977, 1995 by The Lockman Foundation. Used by permission. (www.Lockman.org).

SELF-STUDY BIBLE COURSE
Updated and expanded edition

This book is based on text from *Self Study Bible Course* © 1969 and
In Search of Truth © 1988 by Derek Prince Ministries, International.

Derek Prince Ministries
P.O. Box 19501
Charlotte, NC 28219-9501
www.derekprince.org

ISBN-13: 978-0-88368-750-5
Printed in the United States of America
© 1969, 2005 by Derek Prince Ministries, International

Whitaker House
1030 Hunt Valley Circle
New Kensington, PA 15068
www.whitakerhouse.com

Library of Congress Cataloging-in-Publication Data

Prince, Derek.
  Self-study Bible course / Derek Prince.—Updated and expanded ed.
     p. cm.
  Summary: "Guides the reader on a systematic study of the Bible that explores Christian faith, salvation, healing, the Holy Spirit, worship, prayer, witnessing, and Scripture"—Provided by publisher.
  ISBN-13: 978-0-88368-750-5 (trade pbk. : alk. paper)
  ISBN-10: 0-88368-750-X (trade pbk. : alk. paper) 1. Bible—Textbooks. 2. Bible—Theology. I. Title.

BS605.3.P75 2005
220.6—dc22
                        2005000542

CONTENTS

Introduction: Instructions to the Student 7

Abbreviated Names of Bible Books 11

PART 1: FOUNDATIONS

Study 1
The Bible: The Word of God 15

Study 2
God's Plan of Salvation (Part 1) 23

Study 3
God's Plan of Salvation (Part 2) 31

Study 4
Water Baptism: How? When? Why? 39

Study 5
The Holy Spirit 47

Study 6
Results of the Baptism in the Holy Spirit 55

First Progress Assessment 65

First Review 66

PART 2: DEEPER LIFE

Study 7
Worship and Prayer 69

Study 8
God's Plan for Healing Our Bodies (Part 1) 77

Study 9
God's Plan for Healing Our Bodies (Part 2) 85

Study 10
Witnessing and Winning Souls 93

Study 11
God's Plan for Prosperity 101

Second Progress Assessment 111

Second Review 112

PART 3: ISRAEL: GOD'S CHOSEN PEOPLE

Study 12
God's Special Plan 115

Study 13
Failure and Redemption 125

Study 14
Portrait of Jesus Christ (Part 1) 133

Study 15
Portrait of Jesus Christ (Part 2) 143

Study 16
A Prophet like Moses 153

Third Progress Assessment 163

Third Review 164

PART 4: THE FUTURE

Study 17
The Second Coming of Christ 167

Study 18
Signs of Christ's Second Coming 175

Study 19
Christ's Kingdom Established on Earth 183

Final Progress Assessment... 193

Final Review 194

Study 20
Review and Personal Application.................................. 195

Marks for the Course 199

Glossary...201

About the Author 203

INTRODUCTION: INSTRUCTIONS TO THE STUDENT

Read these instructions before answering any questions.

PURPOSE OF THIS BIBLE COURSE

This self-study course has four main aims:

1. To provide a foundation of Bible knowledge on which to build a strong Christian life.

2. To give you practice in searching the Scriptures and finding God's promises.

3. To train you in analyzing Scripture to find out for yourself its correct meaning.

4. To form in you the habit of accepting spiritual things only if they can be proven in the Bible.

SYSTEM OF BIBLE REFERENCES

The translation of the Bible used throughout this course is the *New King James Version*. The wording in your version may be slightly different. However, the truths taught in this course are equally clear in any reliable version.

To find each book in the Bible and their abbreviated names, look on page 11. Passages of Scripture are given as follows: first, the name of the book; second, the chapter; third, the verse. For example, Rom. 3:23 is Romans, chapter 3, verse 23.

WORD DEFINITIONS

A glossary is included at the back of the book. This gives a simple definition to some of the more difficult words you will encounter in this study. Look at the glossary when you do not know what a word means. Words included in the glossary have an asterisk (*) beside them.

HOW TO DO THE STUDIES

At the start of each study, there is a paragraph headed "Introduction." This gives a brief summary of the main teaching that follows. Always read through the introduction carefully before attempting to answer the questions.

In the first lesson (Study 1: The Bible: The Word of God), there are twenty-four questions. After each question, there are references to one or more Scriptures. The answer to each question is in those Scriptures. Write your answer on the line(s) following each question. Follow these steps:

1. Read the question carefully.

2. Find the Scripture and read it carefully until you find the answer to that question. You may need to read the verses before and after the one given to get the full meaning.

3. Write in simple language the answer you have found.

   Sometimes the answer to one question is divided up into two or more parts. In such cases, the spaces for each part of the answer are numbered.

   Here are the first two questions from Study 1 with the correct answers written in as an example.

1. What name did Jesus give to Scripture? (John 10:35)

   The Word of God
   _____

2. What did Jesus say about the Scripture that shows its authority? (John 10:35)

   It cannot be broken
   _____

   Look up John 10:35 to see if these answers are correct.

MEMORY WORK

At the beginning of each study, there is memory work. You must learn each passage by heart.

Scripture memory cards are printed at the back of this book for your convenience. Carry your memory cards with you wherever you go. Whenever you have a spare moment, review your memory verses. Regular review is the secret of successful memory work. In this way, you will learn the Word by heart. God's Word will give you guidance, strength, spiritual food, victory over the Devil, and seed to sow into the hearts of others.

PROCEDURE FOR WORKING THROUGH THE COURSE

Write in your answer to every question in Study 1, and then—with your Bible closed—write out the memory work in the space provided at the end. Then turn the page to Correct Answers so you can check your work. If your answer does not agree with the correct answer, read the question and the Scripture again until you understand the reason for the correct answer.

On the page after Correct Answers, you will find notes on the correct answers. Read through these notes, and look up the Scriptures that are given.

Finally, mark yourself with the points that you deserve for each answer. If an answer is valued at more than one point, do not allow yourself the full number of points unless your answer is as complete as the correct answer. Remember that the marks for the memory work are important!

Add up your marks for Study 1, and check this total by the standards given at the bottom of the correct answers: 50 percent or higher is "Pass"; 70 percent or higher is "Very Good"; 80 percent or higher is "Excellent."

The method for doing studies 18 and 20 is slightly different but is clearly explained at the beginning of the studies.

Remember! Never turn to the correct answers for any study until you have first written in your own answer to every question in that study—including the memory work!

When you have completed the last study, turn to the page headed "Marks for the Course" (page 199). Write in your marks for each study in the space provided, add them up, and discover your achievement for the course as a whole.

FINAL PERSONAL ADVICE

1. Begin each study with prayer, asking God to guide you and give you understanding.

2. Do not rush. Do not try to accomplish the whole study in one sitting. Read through each passage of Scripture several times until you are sure of its meaning. It will often be helpful to read several verses before or after the Scripture verse given in order to grasp its full meaning.

3. Write neatly and clearly. Do not make your answers longer than necessary. Use a well-sharpened pencil or a ballpoint pen.

4. Pay special attention to the memory work.

5. Pray daily that God may help you to apply in your own life the truths that you are learning.

Abbreviated Names of Bible Books
BOOKS OF THE OLD TESTAMENT

I. The Law
Genesis ....Gen.
Exodus.................................Ex.
Leviticus ....Lev.
Numbers.............................Num.
Deuteronomy.....................Deut.

II. History
Joshua............................... Josh.
Judges................................Judg.
Ruth.................................. Ruth
1 Samuel............................ 1 Sam.
2 Samuel............................ 2 Sam.
1 Kings ....1 Kings
2 Kings ....2 Kings
1 Chronicles ....1 Chron.
2 Chronicles ....2 Chron.
Ezra ....Ezra
Nehemiah...........................Neh.
Esther .... Est.

III. Poetical Books
Job ....Job
Psalms ....Ps.

Proverbs..............................Prov.
Ecclesiastes ....Eccl.
Song of Solomon .... Song

IV. Major Prophets
Isaiah...................................Isa.
Jeremiah..............................Jer.
Lamentations......................Lam.
Ezekiel ....Ezek.
Daniel...................................Dan.

V. Minor Prophets
Hosea ....Hos.
Joel ....Joel
Amos ....Amos
Obadiah.............................. Obad.
Jonah..................................Jonah
Micah .... Mic.
Nahum .... Nah.
Habakkuk........................... Hab.
Zephaniah ....Zeph.
Haggai.................................Hag.
Zechariah ....Zech.
Malachi............................... Mal.

BOOKS OF THE NEW TESTAMENT

I. Gospels
Matthew............................. Matt.
Mark................................... Mark
Luke ....Luke
John....................................John

II. History
Acts.....................................Acts

III. Pauline Epistles
Romans .... Rom.
1 Corinthians ....1 Cor.
2 Corinthians ....2 Cor.
Galatians .... Gal.
Ephesians .... Eph.
Philippians .... Phil.
Colossians........................... Col.
1 Thessalonians............. 1 Thess.

2 Thessalonians............. 2 Thess.
1 Timothy......................... 1 Tim.
2 Timothy......................... 2 Tim.
Titus ....Titus
Philemon ....Philem.
Hebrews.............................. Heb.

IV. General Epistles
James...................................James
1 Peter ....1 Peter
2 Peter ....2 Peter
1 John.................................. 1 John
2 John.................................. 2 John
3 John.................................. 3 John
Jude .... Jude

V. Prophecy
Revelation........................... Rev.

(Note that "John" stands for the gospel of John, but "1 John" for the first epistle of John, and so on.)

PART ONE

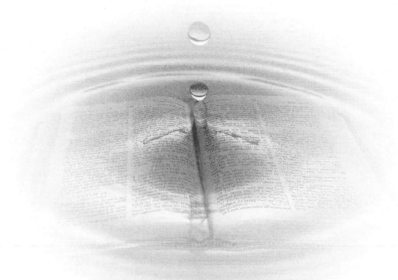

FOUNDATIONS

STUDY ONE
THE BIBLE: THE WORD OF GOD

INTRODUCTION:

The Bible is God's own Word. It is God's great gift to all people everywhere. God gave this gift to help us out of our sin and misery and darkness.

The Bible is not an ordinary book. Every word is true. It is filled with God's own power and authority. The men who wrote it were inspired by the Holy Spirit. God moved them to write the truth exactly as He gave it to them.

We should read our Bibles as if it was God Himself speaking to us—directly and personally. By His Word, God will give us many good things:

- Light
- Understanding
- Spiritual food
- Physical health

The words of the Bible have the power to:

- Cleanse us
- Sanctify* us (set us apart to God)
- Build us up
- Make us sharers in God's own nature
- Give us power and wisdom to overcome the Devil

MEMORY WORK: 2 TIMOTHY 3:16–17

❏ Check here after memorizing the verse.

STUDY QUESTIONS

1. What name did Jesus give to Scripture? (John 10:35)

_____

2. What did Jesus say about the Scripture that shows its authority? (John 10:35)

_____

3. List two things that David tells us about God's Word.

(1) (Ps. 119:89) _____

(2) (Ps. 119:160) _____

4. How were the Scriptures originally given?

(1) (2 Tim. 3:16) _____

(2) (2 Peter 1:20–21) _____

5. What kind of seed must a person receive into his heart in order to be born again and have eternal* life? (1 Peter 1:23)

_____

_____

6. List four things for which the Scriptures are profitable to a Christian.
(2 Tim. 3:16)

(1) _____   (2) _____

(3) _____   (4) _____

7. What is the final result in a Christian who studies and obeys God's Word?
(2 Tim. 3:17)

_____

_____

8. What spiritual food has God provided for His children? (1 Peter 2:2) (Matt. 4:4)

_____

9. How important were God's words to Job? (Job 23:12)

_____

10. When Jeremiah fed on God's Word, what did it become to him? (Jer. 15:16)

_____

11. How can a young Christian person lead a clean life? (Ps. 119:9)

_____

12. Why should a Christian hide (store up) God's Word in his heart? (Ps. 119:11)

_____

13. What two results does God's Word produce in *"young men"* when it lives in them? (1 John 2:14)

   (1) _____

   (2) _____

14. How did Jesus answer the Devil each time He was tempted? (Matt. 4:4, 7, 10)

_____

15. What is the sword that God has given to Christians as part of their spiritual armor? (Eph. 6:17)

_____

16. What two descriptions does Psalm 119 use to show how God's Word helps Christians walk in this world?   (Ps. 119:105)

   (1) _____

   (2) _____

17. What two things does God's Word give to the mind of a Christian? (Ps. 119:130)

   (1) _____   (2) _____

18. What does God's Word provide for the body of a Christian who studies it carefully? (Prov. 4:20–22)

_____

19. When God's people were sick and in need, what did God send to heal and deliver* them? (Ps. 107:20)

_____

20.
List four things from the following verses that God's Word does for His people.

(1) (John 15:3) (Eph. 5:26) _____

(2) (John 17:17) _____

(3) (Acts 20:32) _____

(4) (Acts 20:32) _____

21. How does a Christian prove his love for Christ Jesus? (John 14:21)

_____

22. Whom did Jesus call His mother and His brothers? (Luke 8:21)

_____

23. How is God's love made perfect in a Christian? (1 John 2:5)

_____

24. What two results follow in our lives when we claim the promises of God's Word? (2 Peter 1:4)

(1) _____

(2) _____

MEMORY WORK: 2 TIMOTHY 3:16–17

Write out these verses from memory.

_____

DO NOT TURN THIS PAGE UNTIL YOU HAVE COMPLETED ALL ANSWERS
IN THIS STUDY

CORRECT ANSWERS AND MARKS

STUDY ONE

Question	Answer	Points
1.	The Word of God	1
2.	It cannot be broken	1
3.	(1) It is settled forever in heaven	1
	(2) In its entirety it is truth	1
4.	(1) By inspiration of God	1
	(2) Holy men of God spoke as they were moved by the Holy Spirit	2
5.	The incorruptible (pure) seed of the word of God	2
6.	(1) Doctrine	1
	(2) Reproof (Rebuke)	1
	(3) Correction	1
	(4) Instruction in righteousness*	1
7.	He is made perfect (complete) and thoroughly equipped for every good work	2
8.	The Word of God	1
9.	More than his necessary food	1
10.	The joy and rejoicing of his heart	1
11.	By taking heed according to God's Word	2
12.	That he may not sin against God	1
13.	(1) It makes them strong	1
	(2) They overcome the wicked one (the Devil)	1
14.	He answered from the written Word of God	1
15.	The Word of God	1
16.	(1) It is a lamp to their feet	1
	(2) It is a light to their path	1
17.	(1) Light	1
	(2) Understanding	1
18.	Health to all his flesh	1
19.	He (God) sent His Word	1

20.	(1) It cleanses them (washes, like clean water)	1
	(2) It sanctifies* them	1
	(3) It builds them up (teaches)	1
	(4) It gives them an inheritance	1
21.	He has Christ's commandments and keeps them	2
22.	Those who hear the Word of God and do it	1
23.	By keeping God's Word	1
24.	(1) We are made partakers (sharers) of the divine nature	1
	(2) We escape the corruption of this world	1

Check your memory card for written memory work. 8
If your memory work is word perfect, 4 points for each verse.
(1 point off for each mistake in a verse. If there are more than
3 mistakes, do not mark any points for that verse.)

TOTAL 49

25 correct answers = 50%   34 correct answers = 70%   39 correct answers = 80%

NOTES ON CORRECT ANSWERS
STUDY ONE

(The numbers on this page refer back to the numbers on the Correct Answers page.)

1–2.   Jesus accepted the Old Testament Scriptures. He accepted them without question. He accepted their authority as the inspired Word of God. He based all His teaching on these Scriptures. Jesus spent His entire life obeying these Scriptures and fulfilling them.

3.   God's Word begins in heaven. This Word was given through men. God Himself is the source.

4.   (1) *"By inspiration of God"* (2 Tim. 3:16) means "God inbreathed." The words *breath* and *spirit* are the same in both Hebrew and Greek. (For a full study of the inspiration and authority of the Bible, see *The Spirit-filled Believer's Handbook*, Part I, Foundation for Faith.)

5.   How does the "incorruptible* seed" of God's Word work in us? The seed is received by faith* in the heart. Then it starts growing there by the Holy Spirit. Finally it brings forth divine, eternal*, incorruptible* life. *Incorruptible** means it cannot go bad.

6–8.   Note: *"all scripture"* (2 Tim. 3:16), *"every word"* (Matt. 4:4). To fully learn the Scriptures, a Christian must study the whole Bible and apply the teachings.

8–10.   God's Word provides food for every stage of spiritual development: (1) *"Milk"* for newborn babes (1 Peter 2:2); (2) *"Bread"* for those growing up (Matt. 4:4); (3) *"Solid food"* (full diet) for those who are *"of full age,"* or spiritually mature (Heb. 5:12–14).

11.   We should apply the teaching of God's Word to every part of our lives.

12.   Someone has said, "Either God's Word will keep you from sin, or sin will keep you from God's Word."

13–15.   In Eph. 6:13–17, Paul listed six items of spiritual armor that give the Christian complete protection. But only one of them is a weapon of attack, *"the sword of the Spirit"* (v. 17). It is the responsibility of each believer to *"take"* (v. 17) this sword—which is God's Word.

16.   Look up 1 John 1:7: *"If we walk in the light...."* *"The light"* by which we must walk is God's Word, which enables us to truly see as we walk.

17–19.   God's Word provides for the spirit, mind, and body of the Christian.

20.   (4) Only through God's Word do we come to know (a) what is our rightful inheritance in Christ, and (b) how to obtain that inheritance.

21–23.   "The keeping of God's Word distinguishes you as a disciple of Christ....Your attitude toward God's Word is your attitude toward God Himself. You do not love God more than you love His Word. You do not obey God more than you obey His Word. You do not honor God more than you honor His Word. You do not have more room in your heart and life for God than you have for His Word" (*The Spirit-filled Believer's Handbook*, Part I, Foundation for Faith, Chapter 2).

24.   When we believe and obey God's Word, God's own nature fills our hearts and lives and replaces the old, corrupt Adamic* nature.

STUDY TWO
GOD'S PLAN OF SALVATION (PART 1)

INTRODUCTION:

Sin is an attitude. It is a rebel attitude inside each of us. It rebels against God. Sin turns into outward acts that create distance between us and God. We are all sinners in this way. Our sinful lives rob God of the glory He wants and deserves.

Sin has three results or penalties:

1. Death inside, in our spirit
2. Death of our bodies
3. Being locked up and tortured in a dark place away from God forever

Jesus came to save us from our sins. Jesus Himself never sinned. But He took our sins upon Himself. He died in our place, and He rose again from the dead. Jesus did this so that we might be forgiven and live forever with Him.

MEMORY WORK: ROMANS 6:23

❏ Check here after memorizing the verse. (Review verse from prior lesson daily.)

STUDY QUESTIONS

A. SIN AND ITS CONSEQUENCES

1. Who created all things? (Rev. 4:11)

_____

2. Write down three things that God is worthy to receive. (Rev. 4:11)

(1) _____   (2) _____

(3) _____

3. How many people have sinned? (Rom. 3:23)

_____

4. What were the first two sins that men committed? (Rom. 1:21)

    (1) _____

    (2) _____

5. What were the results of this? (Rom. 1:21)

    (1) In man's mind? _____

    (2) In man's heart? _____

6. Write down two facts about the human heart. (Jer. 17:9)

    (1) _____

    (2) _____

7. Who alone knows the truth about the human heart? (Jer. 17:10) (Luke 16:15)

_____

8. Write down thirteen evil things that come out of the human heart. (Mark 7:21–22)

    (1) _____   (2) _____

    (3) _____   (4) _____

    (5) _____   (6) _____

    (7) _____   (8) _____

    (9) _____   (10) _____

    (11) _____   (12) _____

    (13) _____

9. If we are able to do something good, and we do not do it, what does God call that? (James 4:17)

_____

10.
If we say we have no sin, what are we doing to ourselves? (1 John 1:8)

_____

11. If we say that we have not sinned, what are we doing to God? (1 John 1:10)

_____

12. What penalty has sin brought upon all men? (Rom. 5:12; 6:23) (James 1:15)

_____

13. What is the final end of all who do not repent* of their sins? (Matt. 25:41)
   (Rev. 20:12–15)

_____

14. Write down eight kinds of people who will go to the lake of fire. (Rev. 21:8)

(1) _____   (2) _____

(3) _____   (4) _____

(5) _____   (6) _____

(7) _____   (8) _____

B. THE PURPOSE OF JESUS' DEATH AND RESURRECTION*

15.
For what purpose did Jesus come into the world? (1 Tim. 1:15)

_____

16. Whom did Jesus call, and whom did He receive? (Matt. 9:13) (Luke 15:2)

_____

17. Did Jesus Himself commit any sins? (Heb. 4:15) (1 Peter 2:22)

_____

18. What did Jesus bear for us on the cross? (1 Peter 2:24)

_____

19. For what purpose did Jesus die on the cross? (1 Peter 3:18)

_____

20. What three facts about Jesus did Paul teach as the gospel? (1 Cor. 15:3–4)

    (1) _____

    (2) _____

    (3) _____

21. Seeing that Jesus is now alive forever, what is He able to do for those who come to Him? (Heb. 7:25)

_____

22. Write down three things now offered to all men in the name of Jesus. (Luke 24:47) (Acts 4:12)

    (1) _____   (2) _____

    (3) _____

MEMORY WORK: ROMANS 6:23

Write out this verse from memory.

_____

DO NOT TURN THIS PAGE UNTIL YOU HAVE COMPLETED ALL ANSWERS
IN THIS STUDY

CORRECT ANSWERS AND MARKS
STUDY TWO

Question	Answers	Points
1.	God (the Lord)	1
2.	(1) Glory	1
	(2) Honor	1
	(3) Power	1
3.	All have sinned and fall short of the glory of God	1
4.	(1) They did not glorify* God	1
	(2) They were not thankful	1
5.	(1) They became futile (untrue) in their thoughts	1
	(2) Their foolish hearts were darkened	1
6.	(1) It is deceitful (rotten) above all things	1
	(2) It is desperately (seriously) wicked	1
7.	The Lord (God)	1
8.	(1) Evil thoughts	1
	(2) Adulteries (immoral sex)	1
	(3) Fornications (perverted sex)	1
	(4) Murders	1
	(5) Thefts	1
	(6) Covetousness (greed)	1
	(7) Wickedness	1
	(8) Deceit (cheating)	1
	(9) Lewdness (lust)	1
	(10) An evil eye (envy)	1
	(11) Blasphemy* (cursing)	1
	(12) Pride	1
	(13) Foolishness	1
9.	God calls that sin	1
10.	We deceive (fool) ourselves	1
11.	We make God a liar	1
12.	Death	1
13.	Everlasting fire, the lake of fire, the second death	1

14.	(1) The cowardly (fearful)	1
	(2) The unbelieving	1
	(3) The abominable (hateful)	1
	(4) Murderers	1
	(5) The sexually immoral	1
	(6) Sorcerers (witches)	1
	(7) Idolaters (idol worshipers)	1
	(8) All liars	1
15.	To save sinners	1
16.	Jesus called and received sinners	1
17.	No, none	1
18.	Our sins	1
19.	To bring us to God	1
20.	(1) Jesus died for our sins	1
	(2) He was buried	1
	(3) He rose again the third day	1
21.	To save them to the uttermost (completely)	1
22.	(1) Repentance*	1
	(2) Remission* of sins	1
	(3) Salvation*	1

Check your memory card for written memory work.
If your memory work is word perfect, 4 points.   4
(1 point off for each mistake. If there are more than
3 mistakes, do not mark any points for the verse.)

                                                    TOTAL   54

27 correct answers = 50%   38 correct answers = 70%   43 correct answers = 80%

NOTES ON CORRECT ANSWERS
STUDY TWO

(The numbers on this page refer back to the numbers on the Correct Answers page.)

1–4.　Man's sin is his failure to carry out his God-given duty. Man was created to glorify* God. *"He [man] is the image and glory of God"* (1 Cor. 11:7). Anything that fails to glorify* God is sinful.

3.　*"All...fall short of the glory of God"* (Rom. 3:23). What does this mean? Picture an arrow shot at a mark on a target. The arrow falls short of it. The "mark" for man is to live life to *"the glory of God."* But the Bible says that all have fallen short of this mark. (Look up Philippians 3:14.)

6–8.　All these Scriptures speak about the heart. They show what is inside all men. "All men" means everyone and every human heart.

8.　Not all these sins are committed by all men. But the seeds of all these sins are found in every human heart. Two things work together to decide whether these seeds grow into sin in a person's life: (1) The limits of a person's moral nature, and (2) the people and places in a person's life.

9.　We commit sin by doing something that God forbids. We also sin when we omit, or refuse, to do something God commands. We are just as guilty when we do not do what is good and right. Read Matthew 25:3, 25, 45. They were all condemned for what they did not do. They are the foolish virgins, the unfaithful steward, and the "goat" nations.

13.　There are two different places: (1) Hell (also called Sheol or Hades) is a place where departed souls go before resurrection* and judgment* (Luke 16:23); and (2) Gehenna, or the lake of fire, is the place of punishment after resurrection* and judgment* (Rev. 20:12–15). The lake of fire is the final place of unending torture for wicked people and fallen angels.

14.　Both fearful and unbelieving people are condemned. How many seemingly religious people will be included in that description?

18.　For a time, sin was "covered" by the sacrifices of the law of Moses. (See Hebrews 10:1–4.) But by the death of Jesus, sin was put away forever. (See Hebrews 10:11–18.)

19.　Unforgiven sin separates God and man (Isa. 59:2). Sin was put away by Jesus on the cross. Then the way was opened for man to come back to God. Any bars that now remain are on man's side, not on God's.

20. Faith* is built on fact. The gospel, or good news, is based on these three simple facts that happened in history.

21. *"To the uttermost"* (Heb. 7:25) means "completely." This includes every need of every sinner now and forever. Jesus is more than enough for everyone to the end of time and into eternity*.

STUDY THREE
GOD'S PLAN OF SALVATION (PART 2)

INTRODUCTION:

God now offers salvation* to us through our faith* in Jesus Christ. We are saved through our faith* in Jesus, not through any religion or good works.

To accept God's offer of salvation*, we must do four things:

1. Admit our sins openly and repent* (turn from our sins)

2. Believe that Jesus died for each of us and rose again

3. Receive the risen Christ by faith* as our own personal Savior

4. Publicly confess* Him as our Lord (speak up and tell others that Jesus is Lord)

Here is what happens when we receive Jesus in this way:

• He comes to live forever in our hearts

• He gives us eternal* life

• He gives us the power to lead a life of righteousness*

• He gives us victory over sin

MEMORY WORK: JOHN 1:12–13

❑ Check here after memorizing the verse. (Review verses from prior lessons daily.)

STUDY QUESTIONS

C. HOW WE MAY RECEIVE SALVATION*

23. When should we seek salvation*? (2 Cor. 6:2) (Prov. 27:1)

_____

24. Can we save ourselves by our own good works? (Eph. 2:8–9) (Titus 3:5)

_____

25. Can we be saved by keeping the law? (Rom. 3:20)

_____

26. If we desire God's mercy, what two things must we do? (Prov. 28:13)

(1) _____ (2) _____

27. If we confess* our sins, what two things will God do for us? (1 John 1:9)

(1) _____

(2) _____

28. What is the means God uses to cleanse our hearts from all sin? (1 John 1:7)

_____

29. If we desire to be saved, what two things must we do? (Rom. 10:9–10)

(1) With our hearts? _____

(2) With our mouths? _____

30. If we come to Jesus, will He reject us? (John 6:37)

_____

31. If we open our hearts to receive Jesus, what promise has He given us? (Rev. 3:20)

_____

32. If we receive Jesus, what does He give us? (John 1:12)

_____

33. What experience do we have as a result? (John 1:13) (John 3:3)

_____

34. When we receive Jesus, what does God give us through Him? (Rom. 6:23)

_____

35. Is it possible for us to know we have eternal* life? (1 John 5:13)

_____

36. What record does God give us about Jesus? (1 John 5:11)

_____

37. If we have received Jesus, the Son of God, what do we have? (1 John 5:12–13)

_____

D. SALVATION* GIVES POWER TO OVERCOME THE WORLD AND THE DEVIL

38. After we have received Jesus, who lives in our hearts by faith*? (Gal. 2:20) (Eph. 3:17)

_____

39. What can we do through the strength that Jesus gives us? (Phil. 4:13)

_____

40. If we openly accept or confess* Jesus before men, what will He do for us? (Matt. 10:32)

_____

41. If we deny Jesus before men, what will He do? (Matt. 10:33)

_____

42. What kind of person is able to overcome the world and its temptations?

(1) (1 John 5:4) _____

(2) (1 John 5:5) _____

43. Why are God's children able to overcome the world? (1 John 4:4)

_____

_____

44. By what two things do the people of God overcome the Devil? (Rev. 12:11)

(1) _____

(2) _____

45. Whom has God promised to receive in heaven as His child? (Rev. 21:7)

_____

MEMORY WORK: JOHN 1:12–13

Write out these verses from memory.

_____

DO NOT TURN THIS PAGE UNTIL YOU HAVE COMPLETED ALL ANSWERS
IN THIS STUDY

CORRECT ANSWERS AND MARKS
STUDY THREE

Question	Answers	Points
23.	Now, today	1
24.	No	1
25.	No	1
26.	(1) Confess* our sins	1
	(2) Forsake (leave behind) our sins	1
27.	(1) Forgive us our sins	1
	(2) Cleanse us from all unrighteousness (evil and immoral ways)	1
28.	The blood of Jesus Christ, God's Son	1
29.	(1) Believe that God has raised Jesus from the dead	1
	(2) Confess* Jesus as Lord	1
30.	No	1
31.	"I will come in"	1
32.	The right to become children of God	1
33.	We are born of God (born again)	1
34.	Eternal* life	1
35.	Yes (John wrote for that purpose)	1
36.	God has given us eternal* life in Christ Jesus	2
37.	Eternal* life	1
38.	Christ Jesus lives in our hearts	1
39.	All things (that God wishes us to do)	1
40.	He will confess* us before His heavenly Father	1
41.	He will deny us before His heavenly Father	1
42.	(1) The one who is born of God (through his faith*)	1
	(2) The one who believes that Jesus is the Son of God	1
43.	Because He who is in them (God) is greater than he who is in the world (the Devil)	2

44.	(1) By the blood of the Lamb (Christ Jesus)	1
	(2) By the word of their testimony*	1
45.	He who overcomes	1

Check your memory card for written memory work.

If your memory work is word perfect, 4 points for each verse. 8

(1 point off for each mistake in a verse. If there are more than
3 mistakes, do not mark any points for that verse.)

TOTAL 38

19 correct answers = 50%   27 correct answers =70%   30 correct answers = 80%

NOTES ON CORRECT ANSWERS
STUDY THREE

(The numbers on this page refer back to the numbers on the Correct Answers page.)

24–25. The Bible rules out every attempt by man to save himself or to make himself righteous*. Man cannot be saved without the grace of God. That saving grace is received through faith* in Christ Jesus.

25. The law was not given to make man righteous*. The law was given to show man that he is a sinner and that he cannot save himself. (See Romans 3:20 and Romans 7:7–13.)

26. Just confessing* sin without forsaking it does not gain the mercy of God for man. (Look up and compare Isaiah 55:7.) *Forsake* means to "totally leave behind."

27. When God forgives sin, He also washes and cleans out the sinner's heart. Once the sinner is washed clean, he should not continue in the sins that he has confessed*.

28. Man has no cure of his own for his sinful heart. Only the blood of Christ Jesus can clean out and repair it.

29. (2) "Confess* Jesus as Lord" is a more accurate translation than the *New King James Version*. (Look up and compare 1 Corinthians 12:3 and Philippians 2:11.)

31. The words of Jesus in Revelation 3:20 are addressed to a church at Laodicea. This church claimed to be Christian. But Christ Jesus Himself was left outside their church, seeking to get inside. How many other Christian churches are like this today? Jesus' promise to *"come in"* is made to each of us as individuals. The promise was not made to the church as a whole. Receiving Jesus is always an individual decision.

32. *Right*—or, more correctly, *authority*.

33. John 3:1–7 tells us that we must be born again. John 1:12–13 tells us how we can be born again (of God). It is by receiving Christ Jesus as our personal Savior and Lord.

34. Compare *"wages"* to *"gift"* in Romans 6:23. Notice the contrast: *"wages"* = the just payment for the sins we have committed; *"gift"* = the free, undeserved bestowal of God's grace.

38. The Christian life continues, as it begins, by faith*. *"As you therefore have received Christ Jesus the Lord, so walk in Him"* (Col. 2:6). We receive Jesus by faith*. We walk in Jesus by faith* (2 Cor. 5:7).

39.   More accurately, Philippians 4:13 reads, *"I can do all things through Christ in me giving me the power."*

40–41.   Jesus is the *"High Priest of our confession*"* (Heb. 3:1). That is, Jesus goes to work as our High Priest. He speaks up for us by name before His Father. But He does this only as far as we confess* Him. If there is no confession*, we have no High Priest to speak up for us. (Compare Hebrews 4:14 and Hebrews 10:21–23.) In the last resort, we have only two choices: to confess* or to deny. There is nothing in between.

44.   *"By the blood of the Lamb and by the word of* [our] *testimony"* (Rev. 12:11). We must testify personally to what the Word of God says the blood of Christ Jesus does for us. Some of the great benefits that come to us through the blood of Jesus are: redemption* (Eph. 1:7), cleansing (1 John 1:7), justification* (Rom. 5:9), and sanctification* (Heb. 13:12).

45.   Compare Romans 12:21. In the end, there are only two choices: either to overcome or to be overcome. Again, there is nothing in between.

STUDY FOUR
WATER BAPTISM: HOW? WHEN? WHY?

INTRODUCTION:

Jesus said, *"He who believes and is baptized will be saved"* (Mark 16:16). God's way of salvation* is still the same: First, believe; then, be baptized.

Believing in Christ produces an inward change in our hearts. Being baptized in water is an outward act of obedience to God. By it we testify. We demonstrate that the change has taken place inside, in our hearts.

Baptism makes us one with Christ in His burial and in His resurrection*. We are separated from the old life of sin and defeat. We come out of the water to lead a new life of righteousness* and victory. This is made possible by God's power in us.

The Scriptures in this study explain very carefully how, when, and why we must be baptized.

MEMORY WORK: ROMANS 6:4

❑ Check here after memorizing the verse. (Review verses from prior lessons daily.)

STUDY QUESTIONS

1. What reason did Jesus Himself give for being baptized? (Matt. 3:15)

_____

2. How did the Holy Spirit show that He was pleased with the baptism of Jesus? (Matt. 3:16)

_____

_____

3. What did God the Father say about Jesus when He was baptized? (Matt. 3:17)

_____

4. Did Jesus go down into the water to be baptized? (Matt. 3:16)

_____

5. If a person wishes to be saved, what did Jesus say he should do after believing the gospel? (Mark 16:16)

_____

6. What did Jesus tell His disciples to do to people before baptizing them? (Matt. 28:19)

_____

7. To whom did Jesus send His disciples with this message? (Matt. 28:19)

_____

8. What does Jesus expect people to do after being baptized? (Matt. 28:20)

_____

_____

9. What did Peter tell people to do before being baptized? (Acts 2:38)

_____

10. How many people did Peter say should be baptized? (Acts 2:38)

_____

11. How did the people act who gladly received God's Word? (Acts 2:41)

_____

12. What did the people of Samaria do after they believed Philip's preaching? (Acts 8:12)

_____

13. What did Philip tell the eunuch he must do before he could be baptized? (Acts 8:37)

_____

14. How did the eunuch answer? (Acts 8:37)

_____

15. Did the eunuch go down into the water to be baptized? (Acts 8:38)

_____

16. How did the eunuch feel after being baptized? (Acts 8:39)

_____

17. After Cornelius and his friends had been saved and had received the Holy Spirit, what did the apostle Peter command them to do next? (Acts 10:44–48)

_____

18. What did the Philippian jailer and his family do after believing Paul's message? (Acts 16:29–33)

_____

19. What did the disciples at Ephesus do after believing Paul's message? (Acts 19:4–5)

_____

20. What two experiences of Christ do we follow when we are baptized? (Rom. 6:4) (Col. 2:12)

(1) _____ (2) _____

21. How does Paul say believers should live after being baptized? (Rom. 6:4)

_____

22. Is there any difference between believers of different races after being baptized? (Gal. 3:26–28)

_____

23. What two examples of water baptism found in the Old Testament are referred to in the New Testament?

    (1) (1 Cor. 10:1–2) (Ex. 14:21–22) _____

    (2) (1 Peter 3:20–21) (Gen. 6–7) _____

MEMORY WORK: ROMANS 6:4

Write out this verse from memory.

DO NOT TURN THIS PAGE UNTIL YOU HAVE COMPLETED ALL ANSWERS
IN THIS STUDY

CORRECT ANSWERS AND MARKS
STUDY FOUR

Question	Answers	Points
1.	Thus it is fitting for us to fulfill all righteousness*	2
2.	He (the Holy Spirit) came down like a dove and alighted upon Him	2
3.	This is My beloved Son, in whom I am well pleased	2
4.	Yes	1
5.	He should be baptized	1
6.	To make disciples	1
7.	To all the nations	1
8.	To do what Jesus commands; to observe all things that He has commanded	2
9.	To repent*	1
10.	Everyone	1
11.	They were baptized	1
12.	They were baptized	1
13.	Believe with all his heart	1
14.	I believe that Jesus Christ is the Son of God	1
15.	Yes	1
16.	He went on his way rejoicing	1
17.	To be baptized	1
18.	They were baptized	1
19.	They were baptized	1
20.	(1) His burial	1
	(2) His rising from the dead (resurrection*)	1
21.	They should walk in newness of life	2
22.	No, there is no difference	1

23.   (1) The Israelites passing through the Red Sea   2

          (2) Noah and his family passing through the flood in the ark   2

Check your memory card for written memory work.

If your memory work is word perfect, 4 points.   4

(1 point off for each mistake. If there are more than

3 mistakes, do not mark any points for the verse.)

                                                      TOTAL   36

18 correct answers = 50%   25 correct answers = 70%   29 correct answers = 80%

NOTES ON CORRECT ANSWERS
STUDY FOUR

(The numbers on this page refer back to the numbers on the Correct Answers page.)

1–4.   John's baptism was a *"baptism of repentance*"* with confession* of sins (Mark 1:4–5). But Jesus had no sins to confess* or repent* of. Rather, by being baptized, Jesus showed obedience to the will of God. By doing this, He set an example for others. Jesus gave this reason: *"Thus it is fitting for us to fulfill all righteousness*"* (Matt. 3:15).

The word *"thus"* refers to Jesus' perfect example of baptism: going down into—and coming up out of—the water. *"It is fitting"* refers to His perfect example of obedience for all sincere believers to follow. *"To fulfill all righteousness*"* gives the perfect reason: to complete all righteousness*.

First, the Christian is made righteous* through his faith* in Christ. Then, he completes this inward righteousness* of faith* by an outward act of obedience—being baptized.

Understood in this way, baptism has the clear-cut approval of all three persons of the Godhead: Father, Son, and Spirit.

5, 6,   Before being baptized, a person should fulfill the following three conditions:
9, 13.   (1) be taught the nature of and the reason for baptism; (2) repent* of his sins; (3) believe in Jesus Christ as the Son of God.

7, 10,   Jesus told His disciples that baptism was to be for *"all the nations."* No nation was
11, 12,   to be left out. To this end, the New Testament shows that all new converts were
17, 18,   always baptized without delay. In most cases, this took place on the actual day
19.   of conversion. Never was there a long delay between conversion and baptism. There is no reason this pattern should not be followed now, as in the early church.

8, 20,   By baptism Christians openly join themselves with Christ in His burial and res-
21.   urrection*. After baptism they are required to lead new lives of righteousness*. New life is made possible by the grace and power of the Holy Spirit.

23.   (1) First Corinthians 10:1–2 presents a double baptism for God's people: *"In the cloud and in the sea."* Baptism *"in the cloud"* is a picture of baptism in the Holy Spirit. Baptism *"in the sea"* is a picture of water baptism.

(2) By faith*, Noah and his family entered into the ark (= Christ). Then, in the ark, they passed through the water of the flood (= baptism). Thus they were saved from God's judgment*. They were separated from the old, ungodly world and led into a totally new life.

STUDY FIVE
THE HOLY SPIRIT

INTRODUCTION:

Jesus depended upon the Holy Spirit in His daily ministry on earth.

The Holy Spirit came down upon Him at the Jordan River. Before that, Jesus never preached a sermon or performed a miracle. After that, everything He did was by the power of the Holy Spirit.

As Jesus was about to go up to heaven, He made a promise to His disciples. He promised that He would send them the Holy Spirit from heaven. He did this so that they also would have the Holy Spirit. This promise was fulfilled on the day of Pentecost when they were all baptized in the Holy Spirit. The Holy Spirit was their Helper and supplied all of their spiritual needs.

NOTE: "Holy Spirit" and "Holy Ghost" are two different ways of saying the same thing. There is no difference in meaning.

MEMORY WORK: ACTS 2:38–39

❑ Check here after memorizing the verse. (Review verses from prior lessons daily.)

STUDY QUESTIONS

1. With what did God the Father anoint Jesus for His earthly ministry? (Acts 10:38)

_____

2. What did John the Baptist see descend upon Jesus? (John 1:32–33)

_____

3. What did Jesus say was upon Him, enabling Him to preach and to minister to those in need? (Luke 4:18)

_____

4. By what power did Jesus say He cast out devils? (Matt. 12:28)

_____

5. Whom did Jesus say He would send to His disciples, from the Father, after He Himself returned to heaven? (John 14:16, 26; 15:26)

_____

6. What other term does Jesus use to describe the Helper? (John 14:17; 15:26)

_____

7. List two things that Jesus says the Holy Spirit will do for the disciples. (John 14:26)

    (1)_____

    (2) _____

8. What other way does Jesus say that the Holy Spirit will help the disciples? (John 16:13)

_____

9. List two ways in which the Holy Spirit will reveal Jesus to His disciples.

    (1) (John 15:26) _____

    (2) (John 16:14)_____

10. When did Jesus say that the disciples would receive power to become witnesses for Him in Jerusalem? (Acts 1:8)

_____

11. What did John the Baptist tell the people that Jesus would do for them? (Mark 1:8)

_____

12. What promise did Jesus give to His disciples just before He went up into heaven? (Acts 1:5)

_____

13. What did Jesus tell His disciples to do until this promise should be fulfilled? (Luke 24:49)

_____

_____

14. On what day did the Holy Spirit come to the disciples, as promised by Jesus? (Acts 2:1–4)

_____

15. Why could the Holy Spirit not be given to the disciples during the earthly ministry of Jesus? (John 7:39)

_____

16. After Jesus had returned to His position of glory at the right hand of God, what did He receive from the Father? (Acts 2:33)

_____

17. How could the unbelievers present know that Jesus had poured out the Holy Spirit upon His disciples? (Acts 2:33)

_____

18. What could these unbelievers hear the disciples doing through the power of the Holy Spirit? (Acts 2:7–11)

_____

19. Upon whom does God promise to pour out His Spirit at the close of this age? (Acts 2:17)

_____

20. To whom does Peter say that the promised gift of the Holy Spirit is made available? (Acts 2:39)

_____

21. What good gift will God the Father give to all His children who ask Him for it? (Luke 11:13)

_____

MEMORY WORK: ACTS 2:38–39

Write out these verses from memory.

_____

DO NOT TURN THIS PAGE UNTIL YOU HAVE COMPLETED ALL ANSWERS
IN THIS STUDY

CORRECT ANSWERS AND MARKS
STUDY FIVE

Question	Answers	Points
1.	With the Holy Spirit and with power	1
2.	The (Holy) Spirit in the form of a dove	1
3.	The Spirit of the Lord	1
4.	By the Spirit of God	1
5.	The Helper (the Holy Spirit)	1
6.	The Spirit of truth	2
7.	(1) He will teach you all things	1
	(2) He will bring to your remembrance all things that I said to you	2
8.	He will guide you into all truth	1
9.	(1) He will testify of Me (Jesus)	1
	(2) He will glorify* Me (Jesus)	1
10.	When the Holy Spirit has come upon you	1
11.	He will baptize you with the Holy Spirit	1
12.	You will be baptized with the Holy Spirit not many days from now	2
13.	But tarry (wait) in the city of Jerusalem until you are endued with (given) power from on high	2
14.	The day of Pentecost (called Shabuoth in Hebrew)	1
15.	Because Jesus was not yet glorified*	1
16.	The promise of the Holy Spirit	1
17.	They could see and hear it	1
18.	They were speaking in the languages of the countries from which the unbelievers had come	2
19.	On all flesh (all people)	1
20.	To you, and to your children, and to all who are afar off, as many as the Lord our God will call	3

21.   The Holy Spirit   1

Check your memory card for written memory work.
If your memory work is word perfect, 4 points for each verse.   8
(1 point off for each mistake in a verse. If there are more than
3 mistakes, do not mark any points for that verse.)
                                                              ___
                                                   TOTAL   38

19 correct answers = 50%   27 correct answers = 70%   30 correct answers = 80%

NOTES ON CORRECT ANSWERS
STUDY FIVE

(The numbers on this page refer back to the numbers on the Correct Answers page.)

1–5. The English word *Christ* is taken from a Greek word meaning "anointed." It is exactly the same as the Hebrew word *Messiah*, which also means "anointed." Jesus became the Messiah, the Anointed One, when the Holy Spirit came down upon Him from heaven. This happened at the Jordan River, after His baptism by John the Baptist.

The title "Christ," or "Messiah," shows us that the earthly ministry of Jesus was made possible by the *anointing* of the Holy Spirit. God desires the same anointing for all Christians. *"Now He who establishes us with you in Christ and has anointed us is God"* (2 Cor. 1:21). *"But the anointing which you have received from Him abides* [lives] *in you"* (1 John 2:27).

Christians are literally the "anointed ones." To be true disciples, Christians must depend upon the Holy Spirit. Jesus Himself depended on the Holy Spirit. Jesus showed us the way.

5–6. Another word used for the Holy Spirit is the "Advocate." An advocate is someone who pleads a case, a lawyer. The same word is used for Jesus in 1 John 2:1. Jesus pleads the cause of the believer in heaven. The Holy Spirit pleads the cause of Christ Jesus on earth through the believer. (See Matthew 10:19–20.)

6–9. In John 16:7, Jesus said, *"It is to your advantage that I go away; for if I do not go away, the Helper will not come to you; but if I depart, I will send Him to you."* When Jesus returned to heaven, He sent the Holy Spirit upon the disciples. Immediately they received a better knowledge and understanding of Jesus. They understood Jesus better than when He was present with them on earth. Thus the Holy Spirit fulfilled His ministry. The Holy Spirit is sent to reveal, interpret, and glorify* the person, work, and message of Christ. This is His ministry to us today.

11. Near the beginning of all four Gospels, John the Baptist points to Jesus as the One who *"will baptize you with the Holy Spirit."* The New Testament places the greatest possible importance on this part of Christ's ministry. The Christian church should do the same.

12–13. The Gospels close—like they open—with the promise of the baptism in the Holy Spirit.

15–16. By His death on the cross, Jesus purchased the gift of the Holy Spirit for every believer. (See Galatians 3:13–14.) After His resurrection* and ascension*, Jesus had the special privilege to receive this gift from the Father and then present it as a gift to His disciples.

17–18. All through the New Testament, the baptism in the Holy Spirit is attested by the supernatural evidence of speaking with other tongues.

18–21. At the close of this age, God has promised that He will pour out the Holy Spirit on all people one last time. Every Christian has the scriptural right to ask for this gift.

STUDY SIX
RESULTS OF THE BAPTISM IN THE HOLY SPIRIT

INTRODUCTION:

The baptism in the Holy Spirit is a gift from heaven. The believer who receives this gift is given supernatural power to witness and serve as a disciple of Jesus.

Believers who receive this gift are marked by their ability to speak or pray in a language that is unknown to them. This mark—or gift—is given by the Holy Spirit. This is why it is sometimes called praying in the Holy Spirit. The Bible also calls it "speaking in other tongues" (Acts 2:4). In the New Testament church, this experience was considered normal for all believers.

By praying in this language, the Christian builds up his own spiritual life. He puts himself in direct and constant communion with God. This opens a heavenly gateway that enables both the gifts and the fruits of the Holy Spirit to be worked out in the life of the believer.

MEMORY WORK: ACTS 2:17–18

❏ Check here after memorizing the verse. (Review verses from prior lessons daily.)

STUDY QUESTIONS

1. What happened to the disciples on the day of Pentecost (called Shabuoth in Hebrew) when they were all filled with the Holy Spirit? (Acts 2:4)

_____

_____

2. Who preached to the people of Samaria to believe in Jesus as Messiah? (Acts 8:12)

_____

3. When Peter and John came down to Samaria, what did they pray for the Christians there? (Acts 8:15)

_____

4. How did the Christians at Samaria receive the Holy Spirit? (Acts 8:17)

_____

5. How did Saul of Tarsus (Paul) receive the Holy Spirit? (Acts 9:17)

_____

6. What happened to all who heard Peter preaching in the house of Cornelius? (Acts 10:44)

_____

7. How did Peter and his friends know that everyone in the house of Cornelius had received the Holy Spirit? (Acts 10:45–46)

_____

8. What question did Paul ask the disciples at Ephesus? (Acts 19:2)

_____

9. When did these disciples at Ephesus receive the Holy Spirit? (Acts 19:6)

_____

10. What happened after the Holy Spirit came on these disciples? (Acts 19:6)

_____

11. How much did Paul say that he himself spoke in tongues? (1 Cor. 14:18)

_____

12. List three things that a Christian does when he speaks in an unknown tongue. (1 Cor. 14:2, 4)

(1) _____   (2) _____

(3) _____

13. If a Christian prays in an unknown tongue, what part of him is then praying? (1 Cor. 14:14)

_____

14. How did Jesus say that true worshipers should worship God? (John 4:23–24)

_____

15. How does Jude exhort Christians to build themselves up in their faith*? (Jude 20)

_____

16. When a Christian speaks in an unknown tongue, what may he pray for next? (1 Cor. 14:13)

_____

17. In a public meeting where there is no interpreter, how may a Christian speak in an unknown tongue? (1 Cor. 14:28)

_____

18. Did Paul say that he wished that all Christians spoke in tongues? (1 Cor. 14:5)

_____

19. How many Christians did Paul say may prophesy*? (1 Cor. 14:31)

_____

20. Should Christians be ignorant about spiritual gifts? (1 Cor. 12:1)

_____

21. List the nine gifts of the Spirit. (1 Cor. 12:8–10)

(1) _____   (2) _____

(3) _____   (4) _____

(5) _____   (6) _____

(7) _____ (8) _____

(9) _____

22. What is the ninefold fruit of the Spirit? (Gal. 5:22–23)

(1) _____ (2) _____

(3) _____ (4) _____

(5) _____ (6) _____

(7) _____ (8) _____

(9) _____

23. Should a Christian have spiritual gifts without spiritual fruit? (1 Cor. 13:1–2)

_____

24. Should a Christian have spiritual fruit without spiritual gifts? (1 Cor. 12:31; 14:1)

_____

25. What are three supernatural things that will happen from the out-pouring of the Holy Spirit at the end of this age? (Acts 2:17)

(1) _____

(2) _____

(3) _____

26. List five different spiritual gifts that a believer may use to comfort fellow believers at a meeting. (1 Cor. 14:26)

(1) _____ (2) _____

(3) _____ (4) _____

(5) _____

MEMORY WORK: ACTS 2:17–18

Write out these verses from memory.

_____

DO NOT TURN THIS PAGE UNTIL YOU HAVE COMPLETED ALL ANSWERS
IN THIS STUDY

CORRECT ANSWERS AND MARKS
STUDY SIX

Question	Answers	Points
1.	They spoke with other tongues as the Spirit gave them utterance	2
2.	Philip	1
3.	That they might receive the Holy Spirit	1
4.	Peter and John laid their hands on them	1
5.	Ananias laid his hands upon him	1
6.	The Holy Spirit fell upon them all	1
7.	They heard them speak with tongues and magnify God	1
8.	Did you receive the Holy Spirit when you believed?	1
9.	When Paul had laid his hands on them	1
10.	They spoke with tongues and prophesied*	1
11.	More than you all (that is, more than all the Christians at Corinth)	1
12.	(1) He speaks to God (not to men)	1
	(2) He speaks mysteries	1
	(3) He edifies (comforts and revives) himself	1
13.	His spirit	1
14.	In spirit and truth	1
15.	By praying in the Holy Spirit	1
16.	That he may interpret (or translate)	1
17.	He may speak to himself and to God	1
18.	Yes	1
19.	All	1
20.	No	1
21.	(1) The word of wisdom	1
	(2) The word of knowledge	1
	(3) Faith*	1
	(4) Gifts of healings	1
	(5) Working of miracles	1

	(6) Prophecy	1
	(7) Discerning (awareness) of spirits	1
	(8) Different kinds of tongues	1
	(9) Interpretation of tongues	1
22.	(1) Love	1
	(2) Joy	1
	(3) Peace	1
	(4) Longsuffering (patience)	1
	(5) Kindness	1
	(6) Goodness	1
	(7) Faithfulness	1
	(8) Gentleness	1
	(9) Self-control	1
23.	No	1
24.	No	1
25.	(1) Your sons and your daughters will prophesy*	1
	(2) Your young men will see visions	1
	(3) Your old men will dream dreams	1
26.	(1) A psalm	1
	(2) A teaching	1
	(3) A tongue	1
	(4) A revelation (spiritual insight)	1
	(5) An interpretation	1

Check your memory card for written memory work.

If your memory work is word perfect, 4 points for each verse.   8

(1 point off for each mistake in a verse. If there are more than
3 mistakes, do not mark any points for that verse.)

TOTAL   59

30 correct answers = 50%   41 correct answers = 70%   47 correct answers = 80%

NOTES ON CORRECT ANSWERS
STUDY SIX

(The numbers on this page refer back to the numbers on the Correct Answers page.)

1. *"For out of the abundance* [overflow] *of the heart the mouth speaks"* (Matt. 12:34). The first outflow of the Holy Spirit is from the believer's mouth.

2–4. Philip ministered to the people of Samaria. A great many of them were saved and healed. But this was not enough for the apostles. They also expected all new believers to receive the baptism in the Holy Spirit. So later, after being saved, the new believers in Samaria were baptized in the Holy Spirit. This came about through the ministry of Peter and John.

5. Note that Ananias is simply called a *"disciple"* (Acts 9:10). Therefore, laying on of hands to impart the Holy Spirit was not for the apostles only. Nor is laying on of hands always needed to impart the Holy Spirit. In Acts 2:2–4 and 10:44–46 the believers received without any laying on of hands.

8–10. At Ephesus, as at Samaria, these disciples received the baptism in the Holy Spirit as a separate experience. It happened after being saved. As in Acts 2:4 and 10:46, their experience resulted in speaking in other languages (and also, in Acts 19:2–6, prophesying*).

11–15. The main use of speaking in another language is for personal worship and prayer. The believer does not understand with his mind what he is saying. But his spirit holds direct communion with God. In this way he is able to edify (build up) himself.

16–17. Through the gift of interpretation, Christians may come to know the meaning of something spoken in an unknown language. Words spoken in public meetings in an unknown language should be interpreted by someone. If there is no one to interpret, the believer may speak in an unknown language *"to himself and to God"* (1 Cor. 14:28).

19. To prophesy* is to speak in words given by the Holy Spirit. But the words are spoken in a language that can be understood by the speaker and the listeners.

21–24. There is a difference between gifts and fruit. A gift is given and received all at once, in a moment. Fruit comes by working and waiting. (See 2 Timothy 2:6.) Think about the difference between a Christmas tree with its gifts and an apple tree with its fruit. Spiritually, gifts are not substitutes for fruit. Fruit is not a substitute for gifts. God wants all Christians to have both. (Note that love is never called a gift.)

25–26. There are many results that come from baptism in the Holy Spirit. There are supernatural gifts and fruit. By these, Christians can minister to one another. All of this is above one's own natural ability or schooling.

FIRST PROGRESS ASSESSMENT

CONGRATULATIONS!

You have now completed the **first six studies**. Consider for a moment what this implies!

You have begun your training in righteousness* by introduction to the following themes:

- The Bible as the Word of God

- God's plan of salvation for all people and how you can enter in and enjoy all its benefits

- The teaching about the importance of water baptism

- The provision of the Holy Spirit and all its benefits

In the process, you have searched the Scriptures for answers to these questions and have looked up more than 170 verses! You have also committed to memory ten important verses of Scripture.

Perhaps, at times, you may have found the going rough. You may have asked yourself, Is it really worth all the time and effort? But that only confirms what Solomon said about the search for wisdom: It is like digging for treasure buried in the earth. (See Proverbs 2:1–5.)

Digging is hard, backbreaking work. It produces aching muscles and blistered hands. It is not strange, therefore, if you have experienced some mental "aches" and "blisters" as you have worked through these first six studies.

On the other hand, you are also developing mental and spiritual "muscles." You are building inner stamina and strength of character. The "aches" and the "blisters" are temporary—they will pass. But the character you are developing will be with you forever. It is an essential basis for future success, no matter what your walk in life.

So don't sacrifice the permanent for the sake of the temporary! Keep on digging! The treasure really is there within your reach.

FIRST REVIEW

Before you go on to the exciting new material that lies ahead, it will both encourage and strengthen you to take stock of all that you have discovered up to now. Here are some helpful ways to do this.

First, read carefully through all the questions of the preceding six studies together with the corresponding correct answers. Check that you know and understand the correct answer to each question.

Second, review all the Scripture verses that you have learned for Memory Work.

Third, read carefully through the following questions and consider how you would answer them. Each question is related in some way to the material you have been studying.

1. How have you applied God's remedy for sin in your own life?

2. What benefits can you expect in your own life as you study and obey God's Word?

3. Describe different ways in which the Holy Spirit can help you in your spiritual life.

4. In what ways is Israel's passing through the Red Sea a pattern for those who follow Jesus in baptism?

Finally, write out on a separate sheet of paper your own answers to the above questions.

*   *   *   *   *

There are no marks allotted for this review. Its purpose is to help you consolidate all that you have been discovering. When you are satisfied that this has been achieved, turn the page to Study 7.

PART TWO

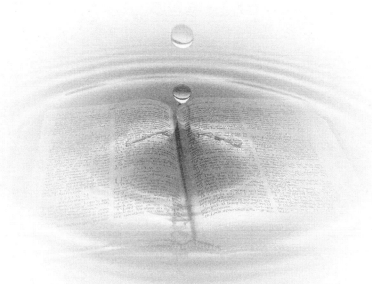

DEEPER LIFE

STUDY SEVEN
WORSHIP AND PRAYER

INTRODUCTION:

Prayer is a way God provided for Christians to come into His presence. Prayer is the way Christians come to receive what they need from God.

Through prayer, Christians receive three things from God.

- Needed guidance
- Help
- Strength for their lives

Christians who want God to hear their prayers must worship Him. Also, all Christians will benefit and be more effective when they set aside dedicated time each day to pray and read the Bible.

The most powerful person in the world is the Christian who knows how to pray and have his prayers answered.

To be able to pray in this way, we must have the help of the Holy Spirit. We must follow carefully the instructions of God's Word. These instructions are set out in this study.

MEMORY WORK: JOHN 15:7

❏ Check here after memorizing the verse. (Review verses from prior lessons daily.)

STUDY QUESTIONS

1. What kind of people is God seeking? (John 4:23–24)

_____

2. In whose prayer does the Lord delight? (Prov. 15:8)

_____

3. What kind of prayer produces great results? (James 5:16)

_____

4. If we wish God to hear our prayers, what two things must we do? (John 9:31)

   (1) _____ (2) _____

5. By what may we enter boldly into the holy presence of God? (Heb. 10:19)

   _____

6. With what two things should we enter God's presence? (Ps. 100:4)

   (1) _____ (2) _____

7. What should a Christian do instead of worrying or being anxious? (Phil. 4:6)

   _____

   _____

8. In whose name should we pray, and with what motive? (John 14:13)

   _____

9. Upon what two conditions may we ask for what we will from God? (John 15:7)

   (1) _____

   (2) _____

10. Write down four things, found in the following verses, that will hinder the answers to our prayers.

    (1) (Ps. 66:18) _____

    (2) (James 1:6–7) _____

    (3) (James 4:3) _____

    (4) (1 Peter 3:7) _____

11. In order to overcome satanic forces, what must we sometimes do when we pray? (Mark 9:29)

    _____

12. In order to receive the things that we desire, what must we do when we pray? (Mark 11:24)

_____

13. If we have anything against other people when we pray, what must we do first? (Mark 11:25)

_____

14. If we forgive others when we pray, how will God deal with us? (Mark 11:25)

_____

15. If we do not forgive others, how will God deal with us? (Mark 11:26)

_____

16. If we pray according to the will of God, of what two things may we be confident? (1 John 5:14–15)

(1) _____

(2) _____

17. How did David say he would begin each day? (Ps. 5:3)

_____

18. At what three times did David decide to pray each day? (Ps. 55:17)

(1) _____   (2) _____

(3) _____

19. Apart from such regular times of prayer, how often should we pray? (Eph. 6:18) (1 Thess. 5:17)

_____

20. When we are weak and do not know how to pray rightly, who helps us to pray in God's will? (Rom. 8:26–27)

_____

21. What steps must we take to pray in private? (Matt. 6:6)

_____

22. How does Jesus say that this kind of prayer will be rewarded? (Matt. 6:6)

_____

23. If we meet with other Christians for prayer in the name of Jesus, what promise has Jesus given us? (Matt. 18:20)

_____

24. What should be our attitude toward other Christians with whom we pray? (Matt. 18:19)

_____

25. For whom should we pray first? (1 Tim. 2:1–2)

_____

26. What position of the body does Paul here suggest for prayer? (1 Tim. 2:8)

_____

27. What two wrong mental attitudes must we guard against when we pray? (1 Tim. 2:8)

(1) _____   (2) _____

28. What is the result of getting our prayers answered? (John 16:24)

_____

MEMORY WORK: JOHN 15:7

Write out this verse from memory.

_____

DO NOT TURN THIS PAGE UNTIL YOU HAVE COMPLETED ALL ANSWERS IN THIS STUDY

CORRECT ANSWERS AND MARKS
Study Seven

Question	Answers	Points
1.	True worshipers, who will worship God in spirit and in truth	2
2.	The prayer of the upright	1
3.	The effective, fervent (fiery) prayer of a righteous* man	2
4.	(1) Worship God	1
	(2) Do God's will	1
5.	By the blood of Jesus	1
6.	(1) Thanksgiving	1
	(2) Praise	1
7.	In everything by prayer and supplication, with thanksgiving, let your requests be made known to God	3
8.	In the name of Jesus, so that God the Father may be glorified*	2
9.	(1) If we abide (live) in Jesus	1
	(2) If His words abide (live) in us	1
10.	(1) If we regard iniquity (permit known sin) in our hearts	1
	(2) If we doubt and do not ask in faith*	1
	(3) If we ask amiss (with a wrong spirit) for our own pleasures	1
	(4) A wrong relationship between husband and wife	1
11.	Fast	1
12.	Believe that we receive them (at the time of praying)	1
13.	We must forgive them	1
14.	God will forgive us	1
15.	God will not forgive us	1
16.	(1) That God hears us	1
	(2) That we have the petitions (requests) that we ask of God	1
17.	By directing his prayer to God and looking up	2
18.	(1) Evening	1
	(2) Morning	1
	(3) Noon	1

19.	Always, without ceasing	1
20.	The Holy Spirit	1
21.	Go into your room, shut the door, and pray in secret	1
22.	Our heavenly Father will reward us openly	1
23.	Jesus is there with us	1
24.	We should agree with them concerning anything that we ask	2
25.	For kings and all who are in authority	1
26.	Lifting up holy hands	1
27.	(1) Wrath	1
	(2) Doubting	1
28.	Joy—full joy	1

Check your memory card for written memory work.
If your memory work is word perfect, 4 points.   4
(1 point off for each mistake. If there are more than
3 mistakes, do not mark any points for the verse.)
                                                           TOTAL   49

25 correct answers = 50%   34 correct answers = 70%   39 correct answers = 80%

NOTES ON CORRECT ANSWERS
STUDY SEVEN

(The numbers on this page refer back to the numbers on the Correct Answers page.)

God is willing and able to answer prayer. The entire Bible—especially the New Testament—show this is true. (See Matthew 7:7–8.) In fact, God is more willing to answer prayer than men are to pray. But, to receive the answers to our prayers, we must meet God's conditions. Most of the answers in this study deal with these conditions. Here is a summary:

5, 8, 23. As sinners, we can go to God only through the atoning sacrifice of Christ Jesus. We rely on Jesus, who speaks for us before His Father. In accepting this fact, we come to God through the name and the blood of Jesus.

1, 4(1), 6, 7. The right approach: worship, thanksgiving, praise.

1, 2, 3, 4(2), 9(1). The right character: truth, uprightness, righteousness*, obedience (all possible only as we abide [live] in Christ).

8, 10(3). The right motive: for God's glory, not to gratify our own lusts. Also, right relationships with other people, especially those closest to us.

10(4), 13, 14, 15, 24, 27(1).

9(2), 16, 25. Praying according to God's will, revealed in His Word.

10(2), 12, 16(2), 27(2). Claim by faith* the answer to our prayers at the actual moment that we pray. *"Now is the accepted time"* (2 Cor. 6:2).

17, 18, 19. Regularity and persistence—don't give up. (Compare Luke 18:1.)

3, 11, 21, 26. Fervency, self-denial, commitment. (Devoting yourself to prayer with a humble heart, alone with God.)

20.   In all this, we cannot rely on just our own will, strength, or understanding. We must have the supernatural help of the Holy Spirit.

22, 28.   The rewards for right praying.

STUDY EIGHT
GOD'S PLAN FOR HEALING OUR BODIES (PART 1)

INTRODUCTION:

When man turned away from God in disobedience, he lost the blessing and protection of God. Man came under a curse and the power of the Devil. Then the Devil was able to bring pain and weakness and sickness to man's body.

However, God in His mercy still desires to bless man. God still wants to save man from his sin and from sickness. Christ Jesus bore our sins and also our sicknesses when He died for us on the cross. This is the good news of salvation*.

Therefore—by faith* in Jesus—we may now receive physical healing for our bodies, as well as forgiveness and peace for our souls.

MEMORY WORK: 1 PETER 2:24

❑ Check here after memorizing the verse. (Review verses from prior lessons daily.)

STUDY QUESTIONS

A. WHO BRINGS SICKNESS AND WHO BRINGS HEALTH?

1. Who first deceived man and tempted him to disobey God? (Gen. 3:1–13) (1 John 3:8) (Rev. 12:9)

_____

2. Why did pain, sickness, and death first come to man? (Gen. 3:14–19)

_____

3. Who brought sickness upon Job? (Job 2:7)

_____

4. Who brought sickness on the woman in Luke 13:11, 16, and how was she bound?

_____

5. Who oppresses* people with sickness? (Acts 10:38)

_____

6. What does God promise to do for His people who obey Him? (Ex. 15:26)

_____

7. What two things does God promise to do for His people who serve Him? (Ex. 23:25)

(1) _____

(2) _____

8. Do sicknesses belong to God's people or to their enemies? (Deut. 7:15)

_____

9. What two things did David say the Lord did for him? (Ps. 103:3)

(1) _____

(2) _____

10. What three things did the apostle John wish for his Christian friend? (3 John 2)

(1)_____

(2) _____

(3) _____

11. How many of God's promises may we claim by saying "yes" and "amen" in Jesus? (2 Cor. 1:19–20)

_____

12. Jesus was manifested (He came into the world) for what purpose? (1 John 3:8)

_____

13. For what purpose did God anoint Jesus with the Holy Spirit? (Acts 10:38)

_____

14. Whose will did Christ Jesus come to do? (John 5:30) (John 6:38)

_____

15. Who worked Jesus' miracles for Him? (John 10:37–38) (John 14:10)

_____

16. How many of those who came to Him did Jesus heal? (Matt. 8:16) (Matt. 12:15) (Matt. 14:35–36) (Luke 4:40) (Luke 6:19)

_____

17. How many kinds of sickness did Jesus heal? (Matt. 4:23–24) (Matt. 9:35)

_____

18. When Jesus did not heal many people, what was the reason? (Matt. 13:58) (Mark 6:5–6)

_____

19. Does God ever change? (Mal. 3:6) (James 1:17)

_____

20. Does Christ Jesus ever change? (Heb. 13:8)

_____

B. The Purpose of Christ's Death on the Cross

21. List three things that Christ Jesus bore in our place. (Matt. 8:17) (1 Peter 2:24)

    (1) _____   (2) _____

    (3) _____

22. As a result, what three outcomes can we have in our lives? (1 Peter 2:24)

(1) _____

(2) _____

(3) _____

23. Who was made a curse in our place? (Gal. 3:13)

_____

24. From what has Jesus redeemed us? (Gal. 3:13)

_____

25. How many kinds of sickness were included in the curse of the law? (Deut. 28:15, 21–22, 27–28, 35, and 59–61)

_____

26. Which does God tell us to choose—blessing or curse? (Deut. 30:19)

_____

MEMORY WORK: 1 PETER 2:24

Write out this verse from memory.

_____

DO NOT TURN THIS PAGE UNTIL YOU HAVE COMPLETED ALL ANSWERS IN THIS STUDY

CORRECT ANSWERS AND MARKS
STUDY EIGHT

Question	Answers	Points
1.	The Serpent, the Devil, Satan	1
2.	Because man disobeyed God	1
3.	Satan—the Devil	1
4.	Satan bound her with a spirit of infirmity	2
5.	The Devil	1
6.	To put none of the diseases of Egypt upon them—to heal them	2
7.	(1) To bless their bread and water	1
	(2) To take sickness away from them	1
8.	To the enemies of God's people	1
9.	(1) The Lord forgave all his iniquities (sins)	1
	(2) The Lord healed all of his diseases	1
10.	(1) That he might prosper	1
	(2) That he might be in health	1
	(3) That his soul might prosper	1
11.	All the promises of God	1
12.	To destroy the works of the Devil	1
13.	To do good and heal all who were oppressed* by the Devil	1
14.	The will of God the Father	1
15.	God the Father	1
16.	All—every one	1
17.	Every kind of sickness and disease	1
18.	The people's unbelief	1
19.	No; never	1
20.	Never	1
21.	(1) Our infirmities	1
	(2) Our sicknesses	1
	(3) Our sins	1

22.   (1) We can be dead to sins   1
      (2) We can live unto righteousness*   1
      (3) We can be healed   1

23.   Jesus   1

24.   The curse of the law   1

25.   Every kind of sickness   1

26.   Blessing   1

Check your memory card for written memory work.
If your memory work is word perfect, 4 points.   4
(1 point off for each mistake. If there are more than
3 mistakes, do not mark any points for that verse.)
                                                                  ─────
                                                   TOTAL   40

20 correct answers = 50%   28 correct answers = 70%   32 correct answers = 80%

NOTES ON CORRECT ANSWERS
STUDY EIGHT

(The numbers on this page refer back to the numbers on the Correct Answers page.)

1–2.   All of Genesis 3 traces the root cause of all human sufferings back to the Devil. Jesus Himself said this about the Devil: *"He was a murderer from the beginning"* (John 8:44).

3–5.   All sickness can be traced back to its source—the Devil. Sickness is part of *"the works of the devil"* (1 John 3:8).

6.   Another way of translating Exodus 15:26 is, "I am Jehovah, your Doctor."

9.   Note the word *"all."* Psalm 103:3 says, *"all your iniquities"* and *"all your diseases."*

10.   Note that John was writing to a model believer, Gaius, who was walking in the truth and doing faithfully his duty as a Christian (3 John 3–5).

11.   Second Corinthians 1:20 goes against the notion that the promise of physical healing is not for Christians today. All the promises of God are (now) for us. That includes all Christians. It means this: "Every promise that fits my situation and meets my need is for me now."

13.   All three persons of the Godhead are actively present in the ministry of healing. The Father anointed the Son with the Spirit. The result was healing for all.

14–15.   The Father's will is perfectly revealed to us in the life of Jesus. This is true for healing and for everything else that Jesus did.

16–18.   Any person who came to Jesus for healing was healed. This is what the Gospels show us in every case.

19–20.   The truth of the gospel is rock-solid and unchanging. The gospel's unchanging truth is based on the unchanging nature of God Himself.

21.   Both Matthew and Peter are quoting from Isaiah 53:4–5. The correct way to read Isaiah 53:4 is, "Surely He has borne our sicknesses and carried our pains." "He" is Christ Jesus. In 1 Peter 2:24, the word *"healed"* is taken from the Greek word that gave us the English word for *doctor*. Truly Jesus is our doctor.

24.   *"The curse of the law"* (Gal. 3:13) means the curse that results from the breaking of the law. This curse is fully described in Deuteronomy 28:15–68. It includes every form of sickness.

26.   God sets forth two opposite pairs. Either (a) life and blessing, or (b) death and cursing. It is left to man to choose.

STUDY NINE
GOD'S PLAN FOR HEALING OUR BODIES
(PART 2)

INTRODUCTION:

Healing for our bodies comes from God. We may receive healing when we:

- Hear God's Word
- Believe God's Word
- Have faith* and allow God's Spirit to fill our bodies with the resurrection* life of Jesus Christ

Even more, we may also offer healing and deliverance* to others in the name of Jesus. Deliverance* is being set free from unclean spirits. There are two main ways of offering healing and deliverance* to others. We may do this by:

- Laying our hands on the sick and praying for them
- Getting believing church elders to anoint them with oil in the name of Jesus

If we act in faith* in this way, God will work with us and confirm the truth of His Word by miracles of healing and deliverance*.

MEMORY WORK: MARK 16:17–18

❏ Check here after memorizing the verse. (Review verses from prior lessons daily.)

STUDY QUESTIONS

C. THREE MEANS OF HEALING:
(1) GOD'S WORD   (2) GOD'S SPIRIT   (3) OUR FAITH*

27. What does God send to heal and deliver* us? (Ps. 107:20)

_____

28. What two benefits do God's words bring to His children? (Prov. 4:20–22)

(1) _____   (2) _____

29. If God's Spirit lives in us, what will it do for our mortal bodies? (Rom. 8:11)

_____

30. What does God want to bring forth (manifest) in our mortal bodies? (2 Cor. 4:10–11)

_____

31. What did Jesus look for in those who came to Him for healing? (Matt. 9:28–29) (Mark 2:5) (Mark 9:23) (Luke 8:50)

_____

32. How did Peter explain the healing of a lame man? (Acts 3:16)

_____

33. What did Paul see in the cripple at Lystra that enabled him to be healed? (Acts 14:8–10)

_____

34. How does faith* come to us? (Rom. 10:17)

_____

D. THE AUTHORITY THAT IS GIVEN TO BELIEVERS

35. Name two types of power that Christ Jesus gave to His disciples. (Matt. 10:1)

(1) _____

(2) _____

36. List four things that Christ Jesus commanded His disciples to do. (Matt. 10:8)

(1) _____   (2) _____

(3) _____   (4) _____

37. When His disciples failed to heal an epileptic, what two reasons did Jesus give? (Matt. 17:20–21) (Mark 9:29)

   (1) _____

   (2) _____

38. Jesus said that a person who believes in Him would be able to do two things. What are they? (John 14:12)

   (1) _____

   (2) _____

39. What may believers do for sick people in the name of Jesus? (Mark 16:17–18)

_____

40. What will happen to these sick people? (Mark 16:18)

_____

41. What should a Christian do when he is sick? (James 5:14)

_____

42. What two things should church elders do for a sick Christian? (James 5:14)

   (1) _____

   (2) _____

43. What two things will the Lord do for a sick Christian? (James 5:15)

   (1) _____

   (2) _____

44. What kind of prayer will save the sick? (James 5:15)

_____

45.

What two things did the disciples pray that God would do in Jesus' name? (Acts 4:29–30)

(1) _____

(2) _____

46. When the disciples went out and preached, what two things did the Lord do for them? (Mark 16:20)

(1) _____

(2) _____

MEMORY WORK: MARK 16:17–18

Write out these verses from memory.

_____

DO NOT TURN THIS PAGE UNTIL YOU HAVE COMPLETED ALL ANSWERS
IN THIS STUDY

CORRECT ANSWERS AND MARKS
STUDY NINE

Question	Answers	Points
27.	His (God's) word	1
28.	(1) Life	1
	(2) Health to all their flesh	1
29.	It will give life to our mortal bodies	1
30.	The life of Jesus	1
31.	Faith* (belief)	1
32.	Faith* in Jesus' name had healed him	2
33.	The cripple had faith* to be healed	1
34.	By hearing the Word of God	2
35.	(1) Power over unclean spirits to cast them out	
2	(2) Power to heal all kinds of sickness and disease	2
36.	(1) To heal the sick	1
	(2) To cleanse the lepers	1
	(3) To raise the dead	1
	(4) To cast out demons	1
37.	(1) Because of their unbelief	1
	(2) It could only come out through prayer and fasting	1
38.	(1) The works that He did	1
	(2) Greater works than these	1
39.	Believers may lay hands on the sick in the name of Jesus	1
40.	They will recover	1
41.	He should call for the elders of the church	1
42.	(1) Pray over him	1
	(2) Anoint him with oil in the name of the Lord Jesus	1
43.	(1) Raise him up	1
	(2) Forgive him if he has committed sins	1
44.	The prayer of faith*	1

45.	(1) Grant that they would speak with boldness	1
	(2) Grant that signs and wonders would be done	1
46.	(1) The Lord worked with them	1
	(2) He confirmed the Word through accompanying signs	2

Check your memory card for written memory work.
If your memory work is word perfect, 4 points for each verse.   8
(1 point off for each mistake in a verse. If there are more than
3 mistakes, do not mark any points for that verse.)

TOTAL   44

22 correct answers = 50%   31 correct answers = 70%   35 correct answers = 80%

NOTES ON CORRECT ANSWERS
STUDY NINE

(The numbers on this page refer back to the numbers on the Correct Answers page.)

27–34.   Psalm 33:6 says that God used His Word and His breath to create the heavens. God's breath is the same as saying God's Spirit. All creation came about by the Word and the Spirit of God working together. The same is true of God's re-creative work of healing. This is done by His Word and His Spirit working together. We receive this work of healing by our faith*.

28.   Proverbs 4:20–22. These verses are God's great "medicine bottle." To be healed, you must take God's medicine as prescribed. Follow His four directions: (1) Give attention to God's words; (2) *"incline your ear"* means to be humble and teachable; (3) keep God's words in front of your eyes; (4) keep God's words in your heart.

   We take God's healing medicine into us through the mind, the ear, the eye, and the heart.

30.   God wants the resurrection* life of Jesus to be *"manifested"* (openly revealed) in our *"mortal flesh"* (2 Cor. 4:10–11). Through Jesus, God gives healing, health, and strength to our bodies in this present life.

34.   Romans 10:17. First, God's Word produces *"hearing."* Then, out of *"hearing"* we develop *"faith*."* The process of hearing is described in its four phases in Proverbs 4:20–21.

35–36.   Think about this: When the disciples were sent out to preach, they were always expected to heal people and to deliver* them from evil spirits. Compare Matthew 10:8 with Matthew 28:20: *"Teaching them to observe all things that I have commanded you; and lo, I am with you always, even to the end of the age."* The *"end of the age"* is this present age. Jesus commanded that this same ministry continue unchanged for each generation of disciples up to the present age. That includes us today, as disciples.

37.   (2) Jesus Himself practiced fasting. He expected His disciples to follow His example. (See Matthew 6:16–18.) However, the disciples did not do this as long as Jesus (the bridegroom) remained with them on earth. (See Mark 2:18–20.)

38.   The ministry of Jesus is the pattern for all Christian ministry. After returning to the Father, Jesus sent the Holy Spirit. The Holy Spirit works today through believing disciples to perform the works promised by Jesus.

39.   The promises of Mark 16:17–18 apply generally to all believers—that is, to *"those who believe."*

39–44.   For further teaching on this subject, see the Laying On of Hands section of my book *The Spirit-filled Believer's Handbook.*

41.   It is our responsibility to call for the elders of the church if we are sick.

45.   Acts 4:30 is still a pattern prayer for the Christian church.

STUDY TEN
WITNESSING AND WINNING SOULS

INTRODUCTION:

By His atoning death on the cross, Jesus made salvation* possible for all men everywhere. But in order to receive salvation*, each person must first hear the Word of God and the testimony of Christ Jesus.

Every person who is saved should be filled with the Holy Spirit. Then they should rely on the power of the Holy Spirit to witness to others about Christ Jesus. If this is done sincerely by every believer, the testimony of Christ will not stop until every part of the earth is reached and all nations have heard. This is God's plan.

This is the great way in which all Christians can work together. We can work to prepare the way for Jesus' return. Christians who are faithful in witnessing will receive a reward from Jesus Himself. In heaven, they will have the joy of seeing the souls who have been won by their testimony. Christians who are not faithful will have to answer to God for lost souls to whom they failed to witness.

MEMORY WORK: ACTS 1:8

❏ Check here after memorizing the verse. (Review verses from prior lessons daily.)

STUDY QUESTIONS

1. What did Jesus tell His disciples that they were to be for Him? (Acts 1:8)

_____

2. How far did Jesus say that His disciples should go as witnesses? (Acts 1:8)

_____

3. To whom must the witness go out to before the end of this age? (Matt. 24:14)

_____

4. Of what three things concerning Jesus did Peter say that he and the other disciples were witnesses? (Acts 10:39–41)

(1) _____   (2) _____

(3) _____

5. What did God tell Paul that he was to do for Christ? (Acts 22:15)

_____

6. What did Paul continue to do from the day he came to know Jesus? (Acts 26:22)

_____

_____

7. What does a true witness do by his testimony? (Prov. 14:25)

_____

8. What should a wise Christian seek to do? (Prov. 11:30)

_____

9. After Andrew found Jesus, whom did he in turn bring to Jesus? (John 1:35–42)

_____

10. After Jesus found Philip, whom did Philip in turn bring to Jesus? (John 1:43–47)

_____

11. When the Pharisees questioned the man born blind, what did he answer from his own experience? (John 9:25)

_____

12. What two truths should we talk about and make known to other people? (1 Chron. 16:8–9)

(1) _____   (2) _____

13. When people opposed Paul's testimony in Corinth, what did God tell Paul? (Acts 18:9)

_____

14. What spirit did Paul tell Timothy was not from God? (2 Tim. 1:7)

_____

15. What does the fear of man bring? (Prov. 29:25)

_____

16. What instruction did Paul give Timothy concerning the testimony of Jesus? (2 Tim. 1:8)

_____

17. When Peter and John were commanded not to speak about Jesus, what two answers did they give?

(1) (Acts 4:20) _____

(2) (Acts 5:29) _____

18. When the other disciples heard that Peter and John had been forbidden to speak about Jesus, what did they all do? (Acts 4:24)

_____

19. After the disciples had prayed and been filled with the Holy Spirit, what did they all do? (Acts 4:31)

_____

20. What special position did God give Ezekiel among his people? (Ezek. 3:17)

_____

21. What did God tell Ezekiel would happen to him if he failed to warn the sinners? (Ezek. 3:18)

_____

22. What two things did Paul testify to all men at Ephesus? (Acts 20:21)

(1) _____

(2) _____

23. Why could Paul say he was pure from the blood of all men at Ephesus? (Acts 20:26–27)

_____

_____

24. What is the final reward laid up for all faithful witnesses of Christ? (2 Tim. 4:8)

_____

MEMORY WORK: ACTS 1:8

Write out this verse from memory.

_____

DO NOT TURN THIS PAGE UNTIL YOU HAVE COMPLETED ALL ANSWERS
IN THIS STUDY

CORRECT ANSWERS AND MARKS
STUDY TEN

Question	Answers	Points
1.	Witnesses	1
2.	To the end of the earth	1
3.	All the world—all the nations	1
4.	(1) All things He did	1
	(2) His death	1
	(3) His resurrection*	1
5.	To be His witness to all men of what he had seen and heard	3
6.	He witnessed to small and great that the Scriptures (the prophets and Moses) were true	3
7.	He delivers* souls	1
8.	Win souls	1
9.	His own brother, Simon	1
10.	Nathanael	1
11.	One thing I know: Though I was blind, now I see	2
12.	(1) God's deeds	1
	(2) His wondrous works	1
13.	Do not be afraid, but speak	2
14.	The spirit of fear	1
15.	A snare	1
16.	Do not be ashamed of the testimony of our Lord	2
17.	(1) We cannot but speak the things which we have seen and heard	2
	(2) We ought to obey God rather than men	1
18.	They raised their voices (prayed) to God with one accord	2
19.	They spoke the Word of God with boldness	1
20.	A watchman	1
21.	God would require their blood at his hand	2

22.   (1) Repentance* toward God   1
        (2) Faith* toward our Lord Jesus Christ   1

23.   Because he had not shunned (run away) from declaring to them   2
        the whole counsel (teaching) of God

24.   A crown of righteousness*   1

Check your memory card for written memory work.
If your memory work is word perfect, 4 points.   4
(1 point off for each mistake. If there are more than
3 mistakes, do not mark any points for that verse.)

                                              TOTAL   44

22 correct answers = 50%   31 correct answers = 70%   35 correct answers = 80%

NOTES ON CORRECT ANSWERS
STUDY TEN

(The numbers on this page refer back to the numbers on the Correct Answers page.)

1. Christians are meant to be witnesses to Christ Himself, not mainly to a doctrine, a denomination, or an experience. Jesus said, *"I, if I am lifted up from the earth, will draw all peoples to Myself"* (John 12:32). Christian testimony should uplift Jesus. To do this effectively, it must be directed and empowered by the Holy Spirit.

4. Compare Acts 1:21–22 and 4:33. The central fact of all testimony about Christ is His resurrection* from the dead.

5–6. Paul's testimony is a pattern for all Christians. It was based on personal experience. It pointed to Christ Jesus. It proved the record of the Scriptures.

7–8. Faithful personal testimony is the most effective way to win other souls to Christ.

9–10. Peter became the leader among the apostles and the chief preacher. But it was his brother Andrew who first came to Christ and brought Peter in turn. Later, Philip brought Nathanael in the same way. So the pattern for winning souls is set by the apostles themselves.

11. Someone has said, "The man with an experience is not at the mercy of the man with an argument." This means that personal experience speaks louder than words alone.

12. A Christian's words should be positive and glorifying* to God. By this he builds up his own faith* and that of others.

13–16, 19. The *"spirit of fear"* (being timid) that Paul wrote about in 2 Timothy 1:7 blocks your ability to testify so that others believe. The Bible teaches clearly that this spirit does not come from God. A Christian should not allow himself to be caught or bound by it. The cure is to be filled with the Holy Spirit.

17(2). The choice between obeying God and obeying man is often clear-cut. The answer of Peter and John is just as valid today.

18. Prayer is the great weapon given to Christians to overcome anything that holds back their testimony.

20–23. When we have a chance to witness to people in our lives, God holds us at fault if we hold back our testimony from them. Ezekiel in the Old Testament and Paul in the New Testament understood this. Paul was required by God to keep back nothing. God wanted Paul to openly speak *"the whole counsel of God"* (Acts 20:27). God still requires the same of Christians today.

STUDY ELEVEN
GOD'S PLAN FOR PROSPERITY

INTRODUCTION:

All through the Bible, God promises to bless and prosper those who trust and serve Him. In order to receive God's financial and material blessings, we must learn to follow God's rule of faith*: *"Give, and it will be given to you"* (Luke 6:38).

We begin by giving back to God. We give the first tenth of all that we receive, in money or in produce. This first tenth, set aside for God, is called our "tithe." Over and above this tithe, we bring our "offerings" to God, as the Holy Spirit directs us. As we do this in faith*, God fully blesses us and supplies all our needs.

MEMORY WORK: MATTHEW 6:33

❑ Check here after memorizing the verse. (Review verses from prior lessons daily.)

STUDY QUESTIONS

A. EXAMPLES OF GOD'S SERVANTS WHO HAVE PROSPERED

1. When God gave Abraham victory in battle, what did Abraham give back to God's priest, Melchizedek? (Gen. 14:19–20)

   _____

2. How did God in turn deal with Abraham? (Gen. 24:1)

   _____

3. What four things did Jacob want God to do for him? (Gen. 28:20)

   (1) _____

   (2) _____

   (3) _____

   (4) _____

4. What did Jacob promise to give God in return? (Gen. 28:22)

_____

5. How did God in turn deal with Jacob? (Gen. 33:11)

_____

6. What kind of man was Joseph? (Gen. 39:2)

_____

7. What was the reason for Joseph's prosperity? (Gen. 39:2, 23)

_____

_____

8. What three things did God command Joshua concerning His law? (Josh. 1:8)

   (1) _____

   (2) _____

   (3) _____

9. What did God promise Joshua if he would do these three things? (Josh. 1:8)

_____

_____

10. What did David promise Solomon if he would obey all the statutes and judgments* of God's law? (1 Chron. 22:13)

_____

11. As long as Uzziah sought the Lord, what did God do for him? (2 Chron. 26:5)

_____

12. When Hezekiah sought and served God with all his heart, what happened to him? (2 Chron. 31:21; 32:30)

_____

B. CONDITIONS AND PROMISES OF PROSPERITY

13. Concerning a certain kind of person, God says that *"whatever he does shall prosper"* (Ps. 1:3).

(a) List three things that such a person must not do. (Ps. 1:1)

(1) _____

(2) _____

(3) _____

(b) Now list two things that such a person must do. (Ps. 1:2)

(1) _____

(2) _____

14. In what two ways did God say that Israel had been robbing Him? (Mal. 3:8)

(1) _____   (2) _____

15.   What happened to Israel as a result of robbing God? (Mal. 3:9)

_____

16. How did God tell Israel to try Him (put Him to the test)? (Mal. 3:10)

_____

17. What did God promise Israel that He would then do for them? (Mal. 3:10)

_____

_____

18. What two things does Jesus tell Christians to seek before all others? (Matt. 6:33)

(1) _____   (2) _____

19. What result does Christ promise will then follow? (Matt. 6:33)

_____

20. When we give, with what measure will it be given back to us? (Luke 6:38)

_____

21. By what standard did Paul tell each Christian to measure how much he should set aside for God? (1 Cor. 16:2)

_____

22. For what purpose did Christ become poor? (2 Cor. 8:9)

_____

_____

23. What kind of person does God love? (2 Cor. 9:7)

_____

24. If we wish to reap bountifully, what must we do first? (2 Cor. 9:6)

_____

25. If God's grace abounds toward us, what two results will follow? (2 Cor. 9:8)

(1) _____

(2) _____

26. From what kind of people will God withhold no good thing? (Ps. 84:11)

_____

27. What kind of people will not lack any good thing? (Ps. 34:10)

_____

28. In what does the Lord take pleasure? (Ps. 35:27)

_____

MEMORY WORK: MATTHEW 6:33

Write out this verse from memory.

_____

DO NOT TURN THIS PAGE UNTIL YOU HAVE COMPLETED ALL ANSWERS
IN THIS STUDY

CORRECT ANSWERS AND MARKS
STUDY ELEVEN

Question	Answers	Points
1.	A tithe (a tenth) of all	1
2.	God blessed Abraham in all things	1
3.	(1) Be with him	1
	(2) Keep him in the way that he went	1
	(3) Give him bread to eat	1
	(4) Give him clothing to put on	1
4.	A tenth of all that God would give him	1
5.	God dealt graciously with Jacob	1
6.	A successful man	1
7.	The Lord was with him and made whatever he did to prosper	1
8.	(1) It should not depart from his mouth	1
	(2) He should meditate* on it day and night	1
	(3) He should observe to do everything that was written in it	1
9.	He would make his way prosperous give him good success	2
10.	Then you will prosper	1
11.	God made him prosper	1
12.	He prospered in all his works	1
13a.	(1) Not walk in the counsel of the ungodly	1
	(2) Not stand in the path of sinners	1
	(3) Not sit in the seat of the scornful	1
13b.	(1) He must delight in the law of the Lord	1
	(2) He must meditate* on the law day and night	1
14.	(1) In tithes	1
	(2) In offerings	1
15.	The whole nation was cursed with a curse	1
16.	By bringing all the tithes into the storehouse	1
17.	Open the windows of heaven and pour out such a blessing that there would not be room enough to receive it all	2

18.	(1) The kingdom of God	1
	(2) The righteousness* of God	1
19.	All these (material) things will be added to them	1
20.	With the same measure that you use to give to others	1
21.	As he may prosper (through God)	1
22.	That through His poverty we might become rich	2
23.	A cheerful giver	1
24.	We must sow bountifully (generously)	1
25.	(1) We will always have all sufficiency (plenty) in all things	1
	(2) We will have an abundance (plenty) for every good work	1
26.	Those who walk uprightly (morally)	1
27.	Those who seek the Lord	1
28.	In the prosperity of His servant	1

Check your memory card for written memory work.
If your memory work is word perfect, 4 points.   4
(1 point off for each mistake. If there are more than
3 mistakes, do not mark any points for that verse.)

TOTAL   47

24 correct answers = 50%   33 correct answers = 70%   38 correct answers = 80%

NOTES ON CORRECT ANSWERS
STUDY ELEVEN

(The numbers on this page refer back to the numbers on the Correct Answers page.)

1–5. Note that tithing did not begin with the Law of Moses. The first person recorded in the Bible as giving tithes is Abraham. In Romans 4:11–12, Abraham is called *"the father of all those who believe…who also walk in the steps of the faith** [of] *our father Abraham."* Believers who give their tithes to God today are certainly walking in the steps of the faith* of Abraham.

Note also that the priest to whom Abraham gave tithes was Melchizedek. And, according to Hebrews 5–7, Jesus is our great High Priest *"according to the order of Melchizedek."* As our High Priest today, Jesus still receives the tithes of His believing people.

Both Abraham and Jacob experienced God's material blessings as a result of their tithing. In Genesis 32:10, Jacob said, *"I crossed over this Jordan with my staff, and now I have become two companies."* When Jacob started to give tithes to God, he owned nothing but the staff in his hand. Twenty years later he was the rich head of a large and growing household.

6–7. Tough straits cannot stop God from keeping His promises. Even in prison Joseph was a success. When he became a great leader in Egypt, he succeeded even more. Joseph's success came from his character and his relationship to God.

8–9. Joshua was called to lead God's people into the Promised Land. Today Christians are called to enter "a land of promises." Then or now, the basis for success is the same. Note that right meditation* is key. Compare the answer to question 13b(2).

10–12. God prospered every king of Judah who was obedient to the law and faithful in the service of the temple—from the time of David to the Babylonian captivity.

13. Note that Psalm 1:1–3 was written to every believer who lives by these words.

14–15. When God's people are not faithful in giving to God, a curse can come on a nation. This is true today for all nations, not just ancient Israel.

16–21. Faith* is the only basis of righteousness* that God will accept. *"Whatever is not from faith* is sin"* (Rom. 14:23). (Compare Hebrews 11:6.) This is true in our handling of money and in every other part of our lives.

22.   According to the Bible, poverty is a curse. Deuteronomy 28:15–68 lists all the curses that result from breaking God's law. In verse 48, the following are included: *"You shall serve your enemies...in hunger, in thirst, in nakedness, and in need of all things."* This is absolute poverty. On the cross, Jesus took upon Himself every one of these curses. (See Galatians 3:13–14.) He was hungry, thirsty, naked, in need of everything. He did this that believers might receive God's riches for every need. (See Philippians 4:19.)

23.   Literally, *"cheerful"* (2 Cor. 9:7) means "hilarious."

24.   Christians should give in the same way that a farmer sows seed. They should give carefully, wisely, in areas that will give the best returns for God's kingdom.

26–28. Prosperity is God's will for His believing people who obey Him.

SECOND PROGRESS ASSESSMENT

CONGRATULATIONS...AGAIN!

You have completed the **first eleven studies**—that's over half of the total course.

The first six studies centered in the salvation message and laid the foundation for your continuing life in Christ. You learned about the significance of water baptism and what it means to be baptized in the Holy Spirit.

In the five studies you just completed, you began the entrance into a deeper life in Christ. Through these studies, you were introduced to the topics of worship, prayer, and witnessing. You were also brought face-to-face with God's provisions for both your physical needs and your financial needs.

Think of it! You now have the answer, not merely for your own deepest needs, but for countless others who are struggling and suffering just as you were. You are no longer part of the problem; you are part of the solution! You can be a light to those around you in darkness. You have moved on from the fundamentals to being able to introduce others to Christ and let them know about your experience.

What a tremendous responsibility! Left to yourself, you could never meet such a challenge. But God has not left you to yourself. He has made full provision for you to lead a life that reflects His grace and glory in every circumstance.

At this point, you have searched the Scriptures and found the answers to 170 specific questions. You have also now committed to memory sixteen verses of Scripture. Your knowledge of the Bible is growing by leaps and bounds!

As you move on to the next five studies, you will begin to see the significance of Israel in the Bible. What was God's plan for His people? You will see how the Old Testament prophecies are fulfilled in the New Testament. And you will see what makes the ministries of Jesus and Moses similar.

SECOND REVIEW

Before going on to the next section of studies, check to see that you fully understand all the material that was covered in studies 7 through 11. As you grasp the meaning of the studies that are already completed, you will be more fitted to go on to the studies that follow.

The method followed in this second review is similar to that of the first.

First, read carefully through all the questions in the preceding eight studies, together with the corresponding correct answers. Check that you now know and understand the correct answer to each question.

Second, review all the passages in these last five studies that you have learned for Memory Work.

Third, carefully read the following questions and consider how you would answer them. Each question is related in some way to the material you have been studying.

1. What scriptural reasons can you give for believing that God still heals those who trust Him today?

2. What three means of healing does God use? How might you take advantage of these?

3. Write out a short testimony of how the Lord has touched your life that you could share with others.

4. Describe briefly the sort of person concerning whom God promises, *"Whatever he does shall prosper"* (Ps. 1:3).

Finally, write out on a separate sheet of paper your own answers to the above questions.

*　*　*　*　*

There are no marks allotted for this second review. Its purpose is to help you take hold of all that you have been discovering. When you are satisfied that this has been achieved, turn the page to Study 12.

PART THREE

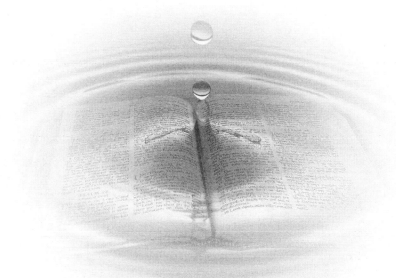

ISRAEL: GOD'S CHOSEN PEOPLE

STUDY TWELVE
GOD'S SPECIAL PLAN

INTRODUCTION:

About 1900 BC God chose a man named Abram (later renamed Abraham) to become the father of a nation for whom He planned a special destiny. God made a covenant with Abraham in which He promised that, through his descendants, all nations would be blessed. God confirmed this covenant to Abraham's son Isaac and to his grandson Jacob (whose name He changed to Israel).

Four hundred and thirty years later, through Moses, God made a further covenant with Jacob's descendants, the nation of Israel, in which He gave them a complete set of laws and a fuller picture of their destiny. Later, God sent prophets to Israel who predicted how their destiny would be worked out.

MEMORY WORK: EXODUS 19:5–6

❏ Check here after memorizing the verse. (Review verses from prior lessons daily.)

STUDY QUESTIONS

A. GOD'S PURPOSE REVEALED TO ABRAHAM

1. How many people did God promise Abraham would be blessed through him? (Gen. 12:3)

_____

2. On what basis did God accept Abraham as righteous*? (Gen. 15:6)

_____

3. To how many people did God promise to make Abraham a father? (Gen. 17:4–5)

_____

4. With whom did God make an everlasting covenant? (Gen. 17:7)

_____

5. What promise did God give to Abraham in this covenant? (Gen. 17:7)

_____

6. Which two descendants of Abraham were later included by name in this covenant? (Ex. 6:3–4) (Lev. 26:42)

_____

7. What new name did God give to Jacob? (Gen. 35:10)

_____

8. What two pictures did God use to show Abraham how numerous his descendants would be? (Gen. 22:17)

(1) _____   (2) _____

9. How many people did God promise Abraham would be blessed in his seed? (Gen. 22:18)

_____

10. Why did God promise this to Abraham? (Gen. 22:18)

_____

11. What did God require Abraham to do for his children and his household in order to receive what God had promised him? (Gen. 18:19)

_____

_____

B. GOD'S PURPOSE REVEALED TO MOSES

12. What were the first two demands that God made on Israel when they came to Mount Sinai? (Ex. 19:5)

(1) _____

(2) _____

13. Provided Israel fulfilled these demands, what three things did God promise they would be? (Ex. 19:5–6)

    (1) _____

    (2) _____

    (3) _____

14. What else did God promise Israel on the same conditions? (Deut. 28:1)

    _____

15. State two ways this would affect the attitude of other peoples toward Israel. (Deut. 28:10)

    (1) _____

    (2) _____

16. What would be the result of Israel's keeping God's covenant? (Deut. 29:9)

    _____

C. God's Purpose Revealed in the Psalms and Prophets

17. What are two ways in which God's favor and blessing on Israel will affect the rest of the world? (Ps. 67:1–2)

    (1) _____

    (2) _____

18. God promises to put His Spirit upon His chosen Servant. What will this Servant do for the Gentiles*? (Isa. 42:1)

    _____

19. State two things that God will appoint this Servant to be for Israel and for the Gentiles*. (Isa. 42:6)

    (1) _____

    (2) _____

20.

What two things did God choose Israel to be for Himself? (Isa. 43:10)

(1) _____ (2) _____

21. Name three ways in which God desired Israel to respond to His revelation of Himself. (Isa. 43:10)

(1) _____ (2) _____

(3) _____

The Prophets give a picture of a future period when God's purposes for Israel will have been fulfilled. The following questions relate to this period.

22. For what two purposes will many people go up to the mountain of the Lord? (Isa. 2:2–3)

(1) _____

(2) _____

23. What two things will go forth from Zion and Jerusalem? (Isa. 2:3)

(1) _____ (2) _____

24. At a time when the people of the earth are in deep darkness, what will the Lord do for Zion? (Isa. 60:2)

_____

25.

How will the other nations and their rulers respond? (Isa. 60:3)

_____

_____

26. At the time when the land of Israel is restored and rebuilt, what two titles will be given to Jews? (Isa. 61:4–6)

(1) _____ (2) _____

27. For what two purposes will many peoples and mighty nations come up to Jerusalem? (Zech. 8:22)

(1) _____ (2) _____

28. What will men from other nations say to a Jew? (Zech. 8:23)

_____

MEMORY WORK: EXODUS 19:5–6

Write out these verses from memory.

_____

DO NOT TURN THIS PAGE UNTIL YOU HAVE COMPLETED ALL ANSWERS IN THIS STUDY

CORRECT ANSWERS AND MARKS
STUDY TWELVE

Question	Answers	Points
1.	All the families of the earth	1
2.	Abraham believed (or believed in) God	1
3.	Many nations	1
4.	With Abraham and his descendants	1
5.	To be God to him and to his descendants	1
6.	Isaac and Jacob	1
7.	Israel	1
8.	(1) The stars of the heaven	1
	(2) The sand on the seashore	1
9.	All the nations of the earth	1
10.	Because Abraham obeyed God's voice	1
11.	To command them to keep the way of the Lord by doing righteousness* and justice	2
12.	(1) To obey God's voice	1
	(2) To keep God's covenant	1
13.	(1) A special treasure to God above all people	1
	(2) A kingdom of priests	1
	(3) A holy nation	1
14.	To set them high above all the nations of the earth	1
15.	(1) They would see that the Israelites are called by the name of the Lord	1
	(2) They would be afraid of Israel	1
16.	They would prosper in all that they did	1
17.	(1) God's way will be known on earth	1
	(2) God's salvation* will be known among all nations	1
18.	He will bring forth justice to the Gentiles*	1
19.	(1) A covenant to the people (Israel)	1
	(2) A light to the Gentiles*	1

20.   (1) His witnesses   1
         (2) His servant   1

21.   (1) To know   1
         (2) To believe   1
         (3) To understand   1

22.   (1) That He may teach them His ways   1
         (2) That they may walk in His paths   1

23.   (1) The law   1
         (2) The word of the Lord   1

24.   He will arise over her and His glory will be seen upon her   2

25.   Gentiles* will come to her light and kings to the brightness of her rising   2

26.   (1) The priests of the Lord   1
         (2) The servants of our God   1

27.   (1) To seek the Lord of hosts   1
         (2) To pray before the Lord   1

28.   Let us go with you, for we have heard that God is with you   2

Check your memory card for written memory work.
If your memory work is word perfect, 4 marks for each verse.   8
(1 point off for each mistake in a verse. If there are more than
3 mistakes, do not mark any points for that verse.)

                                          TOTAL   54

27 correct answers = 50%   38 correct answers = 70%   43 correct answers = 80%

NOTES ON CORRECT ANSWERS
STUDY TWELVE

(The numbers on this page refer back to the numbers on the Correct Answers page.)

1.   From the beginning, God's purpose included all nations on earth.

2.   The basis of Abraham's relationship with God was his faith*.

3.   *Abram* means "exalted father"; *Abraham* means "father of a multitude." From the beginning, God's plan went beyond Abraham's immediate descendants to include people from every nation.

4–5.   A covenant is the most solemn commitment that God can make. Every permanent relationship with God must be based on a covenant. (See Psalm 50:5.)

6–7.   God's covenant was confirmed first to Isaac (not Ishmael); then to Jacob (renamed Israel); then to the nation descended from Jacob and named Israel.

8–9.   God emphasized that the number of people who were to be blessed through Abraham was greater than he could imagine or calculate.

10.   Abraham's faith* was expressed in his obedience—even when that meant sacrificing his son. (See Genesis 22:1–18.)

11.   The way that Abraham instructed and disciplined his household sets God's standard for all fathers. It was the reason why God chose him.

12.   The key to all God's blessings is to obey His voice. (Compare Exodus 15:26 and Deuteronomy 28:1–2.)

13.   These three promises sum up God's purpose for Israel.

14–15. God intended Israel to be a leader and a pattern for all other nations.

16.   See note on question 12.

17.   God intended that the blessings He would bestow on Israel would flow from them to all other nations.

18–19. Ultimately, God's purposes for Israel will be fulfilled through the chosen Servant here described.

20.   See notes on questions 14–15 and 18–19.

21.   This threefold response is necessary for Israel to fulfill God's purpose.

22–23. God intends Jerusalem to be a center of spiritual teaching for all nations.

24–25.   This age will close with a period of worldwide distress and darkness, in the midst of which God will reveal His glory first to Zion and then through Zion to the nations and their rulers.

26.   The restoration of Israel will fulfill God's original purpose, stated in Exodus 19:6.

27–28.   See note on questions 22–23.

STUDY THIRTEEN
FAILURE AND REDEMPTION

INTRODUCTION:

Through Moses, God made a covenant with Israel that had two opposite sides. If Israel would be faithful to the covenant, they would be blessed above all other nations. But if they were unfaithful, God would bring upon them a series of judgments* of ever-increasing severity. In subsequent history, Israel proved unfaithful, and all the judgments* that God predicted came upon them.

However, God promised that, in the latter days, a Redeemer would come to Zion and that Israel would receive forgiveness and cleansing from all their sins and would once more become a holy nation.

MEMORY WORK: ISAIAH 43:25

❏ Check here after memorizing the verse. (Review verses from prior lessons daily.)

STUDY QUESTIONS

A. ISRAEL'S FAILURE

1. What did Moses warn Israel they would do after his death? (Deut. 31:29)

_____

_____

2. Why would disaster come upon Israel in the latter days? (Deut. 31:29)

_____

_____

3. Three times God warned Israel against acting in a certain way toward Him. What was that way? (Lev. 26:21, 23, 27)

_____

4. If Israel refused God's warnings, a series of evil consequences would come upon them. State those described in the following verses of Lev. 26.

(1) v. 25

    (a) _____   (b) _____

    (c) _____

(2) v. 29 _____

(3) v. 31

    (a) _____   (b) _____

    (c) _____

(4) v. 32

    (a) _____   (b) _____

(5) v. 33

    (a) _____   (b) _____

5. Of all the troubles listed in the answers to questions 1 through 4 above, how many have actually come upon the Jewish people?

_____

6. Daniel confessed* various sins committed by his people. What are the ones he specified in Daniel 9:5?

    (1) _____   (2) _____

    (3) _____   (4) _____

    (5) _____

7. In what way had Israel disobeyed the voice of the Lord? (Dan. 9:10)

_____

_____

8. If Daniel were alive today, how many of the same sins would he need to confess* on behalf of the Jewish people?

_____

B. God's Salvation*

9. God warned Israel that they would be driven out of their land but promised that He would not do two things to them. What were they? (Lev. 26:44)

(1) _____

(2) _____

_____

10. What will God remember that will cause Him to show mercy to Israel? (Lev. 26:45)

_____

_____

11. What did David pray to come out of Zion? (Ps. 14:7)

_____

12. In the day when God's anger is turned away, what will Israel say concerning God's salvation*? (Isa. 12:1–2)

_____

13. In what two forms does God reveal Himself to Israel? (Isa. 43:3)

(1) _____   (2) _____

14. Is there any other Savior? (Isa. 43:11)

_____

15. What does God promise concerning Israel's transgressions*? (Isa. 43:25)

_____

16. What does God promise concerning Israel's sins? (Isa. 43:25)

_____

17. To whom in Zion does God promise a Redeemer? (Isa. 59:20)

_____

18. What will come to Zion? (Isa. 62:11)

_____

19. What will be with Him? (Isa. 62:11)

_____

20.   What will be before Him? (Isa. 62:11)

_____

21. In the day when God restores Israel, in what two ways will He deal with their iniquities? (Jer. 33:7–8)

(1) _____   (2) _____

22. In the day when God brings Israel back to their own land, how will He reveal Himself through them to the nations? (Ezek. 39:27)

_____

MEMORY WORK: ISAIAH 43:25

Write out this verse from memory.

_____

DO NOT TURN THIS PAGE UNTIL YOU HAVE COMPLETED ALL ANSWERS IN THIS STUDY.

CORRECT ANSWERS AND MARKS
STUDY THIRTEEN

Question	Answers	Points
1.	Become utterly corrupt and turn from the way Moses commanded them	2
2.	Because they would do evil in the sight of the Lord and provoke Him to anger with the work of their hands	2
3.	Walking contrary to God	1
4.	(1) (a) A sword (war) against them	1
	(b) Struck with pestilence	1
	(c) Delivered into enemy's hands	1
	(2) Eat their own children during the siege	1
	(3) (a) Cities laid waste	1
	(b) Sanctuaries destroyed	1
	(c) No more offerings to the Lord	1
	(4) (a) Land left desolate	1
	(b) Enemies dwell in Israelite's land and are astonished at it	1
	(5) (a) Scattered among the nations	1
	(b) Pursued by the sword	1
5.	All	1
6.	(1) We have sinned	1
	(2) We have committed iniquity	1
	(3) We have done wickedly	1
	(4) We have rebelled	1
	(5) We have departed from God's precepts and judgments*	1
7.	They had not walked in His laws, which He set before them by His prophets	2
8.	All	1
9.	(1) Not cast them away	1
	(2) Not abhor them nor destroy them and break His covenant with them	2
10.	The covenant of their ancestors whom He brought out of the land of Egypt	2
11.	The salvation* of Israel	1
12.	God is/has become my salvation*	1

13.	(1) Their Holy One	1
	(2) Their Savior	1
14.	No	1
15.	He will blot them out	1
16.	He will not remember them	1
17.	To those who turn from transgression* in Jacob	1
18.	Salvation*	1
19.	His reward	1
20.	His work (recompense*)	1
21.	(1) He will cleanse them	1
	(2) He will pardon them	1
22.	He will be hallowed* in them	1

Check your memory card for written memory work.
If your memory work is word perfect, 4 points.   4
(1 point off for each mistake. If there are more than
3 mistakes, do not mark any points for the verse.)

                                                    TOTAL   48

24 correct answers = 50%   34 correct answers = 70%   38 correct answers = 80%

NOTES ON CORRECT ANSWERS
STUDY THIRTEEN

(The numbers on this page refer back to the numbers on the Correct Answers page.)

1–2.   Even before God gave Israel the covenant, He knew that they would break it. He had also prepared a way by which they could receive forgiveness and restoration.

3.   The root of Israel's wrong acts was a wrong attitude: walking contrary to God. Another translation says, "*act*[ing] *with hostility against* [God]" (Lev. 21:26 NASB).

4–5.   The exact way in which these evil consequences came upon Israel is recorded partly in the Bible and partly in the writings of Josephus. They have continued also in later history.

6–8.   The sins confessed* by Daniel can be summed up in one word: rebellion.

9.   God warned Israel that He would punish all their misdeeds, but He also promised that He would never finally reject them as His people. (Compare Jeremiah 33:23–26.)

10.   Even though God's people may be unfaithful, God remains faithful to His covenant. (Compare Psalm 89:34.)

11–14.   God's remedy for Israel's failure is summed up in one word: salvation*. Only God Himself can be a Savior without compromising His own holiness.

15–16.   God's salvation* is so complete that He blots out our sins so that He no longer remembers them.

17.   God, in His mercy, offers Israel a Redeemer, but Israel must respond by turning from their transgressions*.

18–20.   This Redeemer brings three things with Him: salvation*, a reward, and a recompense*.

21.   Salvation* includes both cleansing and pardon.

22.   From the beginning, God's purpose has been to make Israel a blessing to the other nations and to reveal His holiness through Israel.

STUDY FOURTEEN
PORTRAIT OF JESUS CHRIST (PART 1)

INTRODUCTION:

God foresaw that Israel would turn aside into sin and so fail to fulfill His purpose for them. In His mercy, however, He promised to send them a Redeemer from the seed of David. Like David, this Redeemer would be anointed with God's Holy Spirit and for this reason would be known as "Messiah" (Anointed One). In the New Testament, *Christ* means exactly the same as *Messiah*. The coming of this Messiah is a central theme of the Old Testament. (In Hebrew, the Old Testament is called the Tanach.) The prophets describe very exactly how He would come and what He would do.

In the first century, Jewish writers who believed these promises described a man who fulfilled them and whom they acknowledged as Messiah. Their writings were collected in the New Testament. The questions in this study refer partly to the Old Testament and partly to the New Testament.

MEMORY WORK: MALACHI 3:1

❏ Check here after memorizing the verse. (Review verses from prior lessons daily.)

STUDY QUESTIONS

A. MESSIAH'S GENEALOGY

1. To whom did God promise a special seed? (Gen. 22:15–18)

_____

2. What did God promise to all nations through this seed? (Gen. 22:18)

_____

3. Was Jesus descended from this ancestor? (Matt. 1:1)

_____

4. What is now offered through Jesus to the Gentiles*? (Gal. 3:13–14)

_____

5. Through which of Abraham's two sons was the promised seed to come? (Gen. 17:19, 21)

_____

6. Was Jesus descended from Isaac? (Matt. 1:2)

_____

7. To which of his sons did Isaac transmit the blessing of Abraham? (Gen. 28:1–4)

_____

8. Was this blessing extended also to this son's descendants? (Gen. 28:4)

_____

9. Was Jesus descended from Jacob? (Luke 3:34)

_____

10. From which tribe of Israel was the ruler (Messiah) to come? (Gen. 49:10)

_____

11. From which tribe did Jesus come? (Luke 3:33)

_____

12. From which king of Israel was Messiah to be descended? (Ps. 89:35–36) (Isa. 9:6–7)

_____

13. Was Jesus descended from this king? (Matt. 1:6–16)

_____

B. MESSIAH'S BIRTH

14. Where was Messiah to be born? (Mic. 5:2)

_____

15.   Where was Jesus born? (Matt. 2:1) (Luke 2:4–7)

_____

16. What was to be unique about the birth of Messiah? (Isa. 7:14)

_____

17. What was unique about the birth of Jesus? (Matt. 1:18, 22–23) (Luke 1:26–35)

_____

18. Did Daniel provide a way to calculate when Messiah would come? (Dan. 9:25–26)

_____

19. How long after the decree to rebuild Jerusalem was Messiah to come? (Dan. 9:25)

_____

20.   Did Jesus come at the time predicted by Daniel?

_____

C. MESSIAH'S MINISTRY

21. Was any messenger to precede the Messiah? (Mal. 3:1)

_____

22. What was to be the task of this messenger? (Mal. 3:1)

_____

23. Which messenger preceded Jesus? (Matt. 3:1–3; 11:7–10)

_____

24. What was the task of this messenger? (Matt. 3:1–3; 11:7–10) (Luke 1:76)

_____

25. Of what was the Lord to come as a messenger? (Mal. 3:1)

_____

26. Did God promise a new covenant to Israel? (Jer. 31:31–34)

_____

27. Does that covenant provide for complete forgiveness of sins? (Jer. 31:34)

_____

28. Did Jesus come to mediate such a covenant? (Heb. 9:13–15)

_____

29. What did John the Baptist see descending upon Jesus in the form of a dove? (John 1:29–33)

_____

30. Isaiah depicts a man anointed by the Holy Spirit. State four things this anointing would enable him to do. (Isa. 61:1)

(1) _____

(2) _____

(3) _____

(4) _____

31. After reading these words in the synagogue, what did Jesus say about Himself? (Luke 4:16–21)

_____

32. With what did God anoint Jesus of Nazareth? (Acts 10:38)

_____

33. State two things that this anointing enabled Jesus to do. (Acts 10:38)

    (1) _____ \

    (2) _____

34. Isaiah predicted that God would come to save Israel and would bring healing of four types of sickness. List these four types. (Isa. 35:4–6)

    (1) _____   (2) _____

    (3) _____   (4) _____

35. List four types of sickness that Jesus healed. (Mark 8:22–25; 7:32–37) (John 5:5–9) (Matt. 9:32–33)

    (1) _____   (2) _____

    (3) _____   (4) _____

36. Upon what animal was Messiah to ride into Jerusalem? (Zech. 9:9)

    _____

37. Upon what animal (or animals) did the disciples place Jesus for His triumphal entry into Jerusalem? (Matt. 21:6–11) (Mark 11:1–11)

    _____

MEMORY WORK: MALACHI 3:1

Write out this verse from memory.

DO NOT TURN THIS PAGE UNTIL YOU HAVE COMPLETED ALL ANSWERS
IN THIS STUDY

CORRECT ANSWERS AND MARKS
STUDY FOURTEEN

Question	Answers	Points
1.	To Abraham	1
2.	Blessing	1
3.	Yes	1
4.	The blessing of Abraham	1
5.	Isaac	1
6.	Yes	1
7.	Jacob	1
8.	Yes	1
9.	Yes	1
10.	Judah	1
11.	Judah	1
12.	David	1
13.	Yes	1
14.	Bethlehem of Judah	1
15.	Bethlehem of Judah	1
16.	He was to be born of a virgin	1
17.	He was born of a virgin	1
18.	Yes	1
19.	69 weeks (or a total of 483 Jewish years)	1
20.	Yes	1
21.	Yes	1
22.	To prepare the way before Messiah	1
23.	John the Baptist	1
24.	To prepare the way before Jesus	1
25.	The covenant	1
26.	Yes	1

27.	Yes	1
28.	Yes	1
29.	The Holy Spirit	1

30. (1) To preach good tidings to the poor   1
      (2) To heal the brokenhearted   1
      (3) To proclaim liberty to the captives   1
      (4) To open the prison to those who are bound   1

31. Today this Scripture is fulfilled in your hearing   1

32. With the Holy Spirit and with power   1

33. (1) To go about doing good   1
      (2) To heal all who were oppressed* by the Devil   1

34. (1) Blindness   1
      (2) Deafness   1
      (3) Lameness   1
      (4) Dumbness (Muteness)   1

35. (1) Blindness   1
      (2) Deafness   1
      (3) Lameness   1
      (4) Dumbness (Muteness)   1

36. On a donkey, a colt, the foal of a donkey   1

37. On a donkey, a colt, the foal of a donkey   1

Check your memory card for written memory work.
If your Memory Work is word perfect, 4 points.   4
(1 point off for each mistake. If there are more than
3 mistakes, do not mark any points for the verse.)

TOTAL   51

26 correct answers = 50%   36 correct answers = 70%   41 correct answers = 80%

NOTES ON CORRECT ANSWERS
STUDY FOURTEEN

(The numbers on this page refer back to the numbers on the Correct Answers page.)

1–6.   God promised Abraham that through Isaac He would give him a posterity through whom blessing would come to all nations. Jesus, the Messiah, descended from Abraham through Isaac, was the Seed through whom the promise of blessing to all nations was fulfilled. (See Galatians 3:16.)

7–9.   The promise of the Seed through whom blessing was to come was passed down through Jacob. Thus, Messiah had to come from the line of the Jewish people.

10–13.   God ordained that the ruler of Israel should come from the tribe of Judah. This was fulfilled first in David and then in Jesus, who was descended from David.

1–13.   No one challenged the genealogy or the Davidic ancestry of Jesus while He was on earth. All Israel's genealogical records perished when the second temple was destroyed in 70 AD. It is therefore impossible for anyone born after that date to prove His claim to be Messiah.

In Luke's genealogy of Jesus, he said only that Jesus was supposed to be the son of Joseph. (See Luke 3:23.)

14–15.   At the time of the birth of Jesus, the Jewish religious leaders were expecting the Messiah to be born in Bethlehem of Judah. (See Matthew 2:1–6.)

16–17.   Note the following reasons for translating *almah* in this passage as *"virgin"* (Isa. 7:14): (1) The Jewish writers of the Septuagint translated it *parthenos*, the standard Greek word for *virgin*; (2) No prophecy of the Tanach refers to a human father of Messiah, only to a mother (see Isaiah 49:1, 5; Psalm 22:9); (3) *Almah* describes a young woman, not yet married, which applied exactly to Mary; (4) In the Tanach, *almah* is used only to refer to a virgin (see Genesis 24:43; Exodus 2:8); (5) The alternative Hebrew word *bethulah* in Joel 1:8 refers to a woman who has had a husband. Moreover, *bethulah* is sometimes used to personify a nation (see Isaiah 23:12; 47:1; Jeremiah 18:13; 31:4, 21).

18–20.   According to Daniel 9:25–26, Messiah would come and then be cut off after 69 weeks (literally, "sevens") of years. Since the Jewish year is equivalent to 360 days, the actual number according to the Western calendar would be about 477 years. The decree to restore Jerusalem in the reign of Artaxerxes

King of Persia was probably issued about 445 BC. This would give a date of about 32 AD for the coming of Messiah the Prince. Jesus made His triumphal entry into Jerusalem about that time and shortly afterward was *"cut off." "The people of the prince who is to come"* were the Roman legions under Titus who destroyed Jerusalem in 70 AD.

25–28. The new covenant promised in Jeremiah 31:31–34 has three main features: (1) a new inner nature (*"I will put My law in their minds, and write it on their hearts"*); (2) a personal relationship with God (*"they all shall know Me"*); (3) forgiveness of sins (*"I will forgive their iniquity, and their sin I will remember no more"*). These features are all included in the covenant that Jesus instituted. Also, in Ezekiel 16:59–60, God charges Israel with breaking the first covenant but promises to replace it with an everlasting covenant.

29–35. The Holy Spirit coming down upon Jesus marked Him out as the promised Messiah. This equipped Him to be the deliverer of God's people from both sin and sickness.

34–35. The healing miracles of Jesus confirmed His identity as Messiah.

36–37. It was customary for a king to ride upon a donkey. (See 1 Kings 1:33–34.)

STUDY FIFTEEN
PORTRAIT OF JESUS CHRIST (PART 2)

INTRODUCTION:

The apostle Peter wrote concerning the prophets of the Old Testament that the Spirit of Christ within them predicted the sufferings of Christ and the glory that was to follow (1 Peter 1:10–11). At times, these prophets spoke in the first person of going through experiences that never actually happened to them but that did happen later in the life of Jesus. They described first the sufferings of Christ (Messiah) and then the eternal* glory into which He was to enter. Such predictions occur most frequently in the Psalms of David and in Isaiah. This study contains various examples.

MEMORY WORK: ISAIAH 53:4–5

❏ Check here after memorizing the verse. (Review verses from prior lessons daily.)

STUDY QUESTIONS

D. MESSIAH'S SUFFERING

38. Was Messiah to be accepted or rejected by His own people? (Isa. 53:1–3)

_____

39. Did Israel as a nation accept or reject Jesus? (John 1:11; 12:37–38)

_____

40.
By what kind of person was Messiah to be betrayed? (Ps. 41:9)

_____

41. By whom was Jesus betrayed? (Mark 14:10)

_____

42. Was this man a friend of Jesus? (Matt. 26:47, 50)

_____

43. For what price was Messiah to be betrayed? (Zech. 11:12)

_____

44. How much money did Jesus' betrayer receive? (Matt. 26:15)

_____

45. What was to be done with the money of Messiah's betrayal? (Zech. 11:13)

_____

_____

46. What was done with the money of Jesus' betrayal? (Matt. 27:3–7)

_____

_____

47. Was Messiah to defend Himself before His accusers? (Isa. 53:7)

_____

48. How did Jesus react to His accusers? (Matt. 26:62–63; 27:12–14)

_____

49. Was Messiah to be beaten and spat upon? (Isa. 50:6)

_____

50. Name two ways in which Jesus suffered at the hands of His oppressors*. (Mark 14:65) (John 19:1)

_____

51. What kind of people were to be executed together with Messiah? (Isa. 53:12)

_____

52. Who were the two men crucified together with Jesus? (Matt. 27:38)

_____

53. Name two parts of Messiah's body that were to be pierced. (Ps. 22:16)

_____

54. Was Jesus pierced in His hands and feet? (Luke 24:39–40) (John 20:25–27)

_____

55. What was to happen to Messiah's garments and clothing? (Ps. 22:18)

_____

56. What did the Roman soldiers do with the garments and tunic of Jesus? (John 19:23–24)

_____

57. What were they to give Messiah to drink? (Ps. 69:21)

_____

58. What did they give Jesus to drink? (John 19:29)

_____

59. What could not happen to Messiah's bones? (Ps. 34:19–20)

_____

60. Were the bones of Jesus broken? (John 19:33, 36)

_____

61. What was the Lord to lay upon Messiah? (Isa. 53:6)

_____

62. What was to happen to Messiah as a result? (Isa. 53:8)

_____

63. What did Jesus bear on the cross? (1 Peter 2:24)

_____

64. What happened to Jesus as a result? (1 Peter 3:18)

_____

65.
In the tomb of what kind of person was Messiah to be buried? (Isa. 53:9)

_____

66. In whose tomb was Jesus buried? (Matt. 27:57–60)

_____

67. What kind of person was he? (Matt. 27:57)

_____

E. Messiah's Victory over Death

68. After Messiah's soul had become a sin offering, what three things are promised concerning Him? (Isa. 53:10)

   (1) _____   (2) _____

   (3) _____

69. Could these promises have been fulfilled if Messiah had remained dead?

_____

70.
What two things does God promise to His Holy One? (Ps. 16:10)

   (1) _____

   (2) _____

71. Were these two things fulfilled in the experience of David? (1 Kings 2:10) (Acts 2:29)

_____

72. In whose experience were they fulfilled? (Acts 2:30–32)

_____

73. What position of authority did God promise to Messiah? (Ps. 110:1)

_____

74. Could this have been fulfilled as long as He remained on earth?

_____

75. To what place of authority did God exalt Jesus? (Acts 2:33–36)

_____

76. Until what time must Jesus remain in heaven? (Acts 3:19–21)

_____

77. How will Messiah come to establish His kingdom? (Dan. 7:13)

_____

78. How will Jesus return from heaven? (Matt. 26:63–64)

_____

79. On what mountain will Messiah's feet rest? (Zech. 14:4)

_____

80. To what mountain will Jesus return? (Acts 1:9–12)

_____

Memory Work: Isaiah 53:4–5

Write out these verses from memory.

DO NOT TURN THIS PAGE UNTIL YOU HAVE COMPLETED ALL ANSWERS IN THIS STUDY

CORRECT ANSWERS AND MARKS
STUDY FIFTEEN

Question	Answers	Points
38.	He was to be rejected	1
39.	They rejected Him	1
40.	A familiar (or close) friend	1
41.	Judas Iscariot	1
42.	Yes	1
43.	Thirty pieces of silver	1
44.	Thirty pieces of silver	1
45.	It was to be thrown to the potter in the house of the Lord	2
46.	It was thrown down in the temple and used to buy a potter's field	2
47.	No	1
48.	He remained silent	1
49.	Yes	1
50.	He was beaten and spat upon	2
51.	Transgressors*	1
52.	Two robbers (transgressors*)	1
53.	His hands and His feet	2
54.	Yes	1
55.	They were to be divided, and lots were to be cast for them	2
56.	They divided His garments and cast lots for His clothing	2
57.	Vinegar	1
58.	Sour wine (or vinegar)	1
59.	They could not be broken	1
60.	No	1
61.	The iniquity of us all	1
62.	He was to be cut off from the land of the living	2
63.	Our sins	1

64.	He was put to death	1
65.	A rich man	1
66.	Joseph of Arimathea	1
67.	A rich man	1
68.	(1) He will see His seed	1
	(2) He will prolong His days	1
	(3) The pleasure of the Lord will prosper in His hand	1
69.	No	1
70.	(1) He will not leave His soul in Sheol	1
	(2) He will not allow Him to see corruption	1
71.	No	1
72.	The experience of Jesus	1
73.	To sit at God's right hand	1
74.	No	1
75.	God's right hand	1
76.	The times of restoration of all things	1
77.	Coming with clouds of heaven	1
78.	Coming on clouds of heaven	1
79.	The Mount of Olives	1
80.	The Mount of Olives	1

Check your memory card for written memory work.
If your memory work is word perfect, 4 points for each verse.   8
(1 point off for each mistake in a verse. If there are more than
3 mistakes, do not mark any points for that verse.)

TOTAL   61

31 correct answers = 50%   43 correct answers = 70%   49 correct answers = 80%

NOTES ON CORRECT ANSWERS
STUDY FIFTEEN

(The numbers on this page refer back to the numbers on the Correct Answers page.)

38, 47, 51, 61, 62, 65, 68.   Isaiah 52:13 and 53:12 are great Messianic prophecies of the Old Testament. They depict a Servant of the Lord who is rejected by His own people, though without any sin on His part, and who suffers the penalty of death for their iniquities. The Jewish commentators have attempted to identify the *"Servant"* of Isaiah 52:13 as the Jewish people, who have suffered at the hands of other nations. But this interpretation cannot be valid for the following reasons:

1. The *"Servant"* here depicted was not guilty of any violence or deceit. (See Isaiah 53:9.) This does not apply to the Jewish people.

2. The *"Servant"* was wounded for the transgressions* of others. (See verses 4–6.) Israel's sufferings were caused by her own sins, as Moses had warned. (See Leviticus 26:14–43.)

3. By a personal knowledge of this *"Servant"* (who bore the iniquities of others upon Himself), many would be made righteous* before God. This only comes through personal faith* in the Messiah. (See Romans 3:21–24.)

39.   Israel as a nation rejected Jesus. Nevertheless, there was a remnant who followed Him. The early assembly of believers consisted mainly of Messianic Jews.

59–60.   The Passover lamb, by whose blood the children of Israel were protected from the angel of death, could not have any of its bones broken (Ex. 12:46). Jesus, as the sacrificial lamb of God, likewise could not have any bones broken (John 1:29) (1 Cor. 5:7).

61–64.   The sacrifice of Jesus was foreshadowed each Day of Atonement when the high priest transferred Israel's sins to the scapegoat (Lev. 16:21–22). Only the blood of the sacrifice could atone for sin (Lev. 17:11). Therefore, Jesus not only bore the sins of the people but also shed His blood for a full and final atonement (Heb. 9:13–22).

68–72.   The resurrection* of Jesus from the dead was God's vindication of Him as Messiah and Lord (Rom. 1:3–4).

73–75.   Jesus not only rose from the dead but also ascended up to God the Father in heaven. The right hand of God represents the seat of all authority and power in the universe. Jesus has taken His place there, ruling in the midst of His enemies until all things submit to His dominion. (See Psalm 110:2.)

76.   God has promised a period of restoration at the close of this age. This will center in the restoration of Israel and will climax with the return of Messiah in glory. (See Psalm 102:16.)

77–80. The prophecies of Messiah's return in glory are even more numerous than those of His first coming in humility.

STUDY SIXTEEN
A PROPHET LIKE MOSES

INTRODUCTION:

In Deuteronomy 18:18–19, Moses brought to Israel the following promise of God:

I will raise up for them a Prophet like you from among their brethren, and will put My words in His mouth, and He shall speak to them all that I command Him. And it shall be that whoever will not hear My words, which He speaks in My name, I will require it of him.

These words of Moses clearly establish three facts:

First, Moses here described one particular prophet, whom God promises to send to Israel at a later time. The language that Moses used is singular throughout: *"a Prophet," "His mouth," "He shall speak."* These words cannot describe the later prophets in Israel as a whole. They must refer to one special prophet.

Second, this special prophet was to have unique authority, above all others who had gone before him. If anyone in Israel refused to hear this prophet, God would bring judgment* upon that person.

Third, this prophet was to be like Moses in ways that would distinguish him from all other prophets who would ever come to Israel.

In Acts 3:22–26, the apostle Peter quoted these words of Moses and applied them directly to Jesus of Nazareth. A careful comparison of the Old and New Testaments shows over twenty distinct points of resemblance between Moses and Jesus. The following questions regarding the similarities between these two prophets are grouped according to three main headings: Childhood, Personal Experiences, and Ministry.

MEMORY WORK: DEUTERONOMY 18:18

❑ Check here after memorizing the verse. (Review verses from prior lessons daily.)

STUDY QUESTIONS

A. THEIR CHILDHOOD

1. Name the Gentile emperor who imposed his rule on Israel at the time of the birth of each of these prophets. (Ex. 1:8–14) (Luke 2:1–7)

    (1) Moses _____

    (2) Jesus _____

2. How were the lives of both Moses and Jesus endangered in their infancy? (Ex. 1:15–16) (Matt. 2:16)

    _____

3. By whose actions were their lives saved? (Ex. 2:1–5) (Heb. 11:23) (Matt. 2:13–14)

    _____

4. With what people did each find refuge for a time? (Ex. 2:10) (Matt. 2:14–15)

    _____

5. What intellectual ability did each display? (Acts 7:22) (Luke 2:46–47) (Matt. 13:54)

    _____

B. THEIR PERSONAL EXPERIENCES

6. Name two character traits common to each man. (Num. 12:3, 7) (Matt. 11:29) (Heb. 3:1–6)

    (1) _____   (2) _____

7. Were these prophets always received by Israel? (Ex. 2:14; 32:1) (Num. 16:41) (John 7:52) (Matt. 27:21–22)

    _____

8. How did their brothers and sisters react to them at times? (Num. 12:1) (Mark 3:21) (Matt. 13:54–57) (John 7:3–5)

_____

9. How did each prophet respond before God in regard to the sin of Israel? (Ex. 32:31–32) (Luke 23:34)

_____

10. What was each willing to do to placate God's wrath against the sin of the people? (Ex. 32:31–32) (Luke 23:34)

_____

11. What did each of these prophets do at a crucial point in their lives? (Ex. 34:28) (Matt. 4:2)

_____

12. Did each of these prophets enjoy special intimacy with God? (Num. 12:7–8) (John 1:18) (Matt. 11:27)

_____

13. To what kind of place did each of these prophets go to have communion with God? (Ex. 24:12) (Matt. 17:1, 5)

_____

14. Did they take any disciples with them? (Ex. 24:13) (Matt. 17:1)

_____

15. What effect did that experience have on their physical bodies? (Ex. 34:29–30) (Matt. 17:2)

_____

16. In what special way did God speak to them on at least one occasion? (Ex. 19:19–20) (John 12:28–30)

_____

17. Which supernatural beings guarded the burial place of each prophet? (Jude 9) (Matt. 28:2–7)

_____

C. THEIR MINISTRY

18. Name two other ministries, besides that of prophet, that each man exercised.

(1) Deut. 4:1, 5; Matt. 5:1–2; John 3:1–2 _____

(2) Ps. 77:20; Isa. 63:11; John 10:11, 14, 17 _____

19. What special, important truth about God did each reveal to God's people? (Ex. 3:13–15) (John 17:6)

_____

20. What type of food did God supernaturally provide to His people through each of these prophets? (Ex. 16:14–15) (Ps. 78:24) (John 6:32–33, 51)

_____

21. From what kind of slavery did Moses deliver Israel? (Ex. 3:10) (Deut. 6:21)

_____

22. From what kind of slavery did Jesus deliver those who believed in Him? (John 8:31–36)

_____

23. How did both these prophets help the sick? (Ex. 15:25–26) (Num. 21:6–9) (Matt. 4:23; 8:16–17)

_____

24. Was there any other prophet who worked such great miracles as these? (Deut. 34:10–12) (John 5:36; 15:24) (Acts 2:22)

_____

25.

What did each establish between God and His people? (Ex. 24:7–8) (Matt. 26:26–28)

---

26. By what was it sealed? (Heb. 9:11–22)

MEMORY WORK: DEUTERONOMY 18:18

Write out this verse from memory.

DO NOT TURN THIS PAGE UNTIL YOU HAVE COMPLETED ALL ANSWERS
IN THIS STUDY

CORRECT ANSWERS AND MARKS
STUDY SIXTEEN

Question	Answers	Points
1.	(1) Pharaoh	1
	(2) Caesar Augustus	1
2.	Evil kings made decrees for each of them to be killed	1
3.	By the action of their parents	1
4.	The people of Egypt	1
5.	Unusual wisdom and understanding	1
6.	(1) Humility	1
	(2) Faithfulness to God	1
7.	No	1
8.	They criticized/rejected them	1
9.	Each prayed to God to forgive the people	1
10.	Each was willing to bear the punishment of the people	1
11.	Each fasted forty days	1
12.	Yes	1
13.	A high mountain	1
14.	Yes	1
15.	Their faces shone	1
16.	God spoke in an audible voice from heaven	1
17.	Angels	1
18.	(1) Teacher	1
	(2) Shepherd	1
19.	God's name	1
20.	Bread from heaven	1
21.	From slavery to Pharaoh in Egypt	1
22.	From slavery to sin	1
23.	They healed them	1
24.	No	1

25. A covenant   1

26. The blood of a sacrifice (Jesus' crucifixion)   1

Check your memory card for written memory work.
If your memory work is word perfect, 4 points.   4
(1 point off for each mistake. If there are more than
3 mistakes, do not mark any points for the verse.)

                                              TOTAL   33

17 correct answers = 50%   23 correct answers = 70%   26 correct answers = 80%

NOTES ON CORRECT ANSWERS
STUDY SIXTEEN

(The numbers on this page refer back to the numbers on the Correct Answers page.)

1–4.   In each case, Satan, the great enemy of Israel, sought to destroy God's appointed deliverer before he could fulfill his task. Each was preserved through the faith* and courage of his parents.

5.   Both Moses and Jesus were equipped by God with special intellectual gifts.

6.   Both relied on God's supernatural power, not on their own natural strength.

7–8.   Wrong attitudes can keep God's people from recognizing or honoring the deliverer whom God has sent to them.

9–10.   Both Moses and Jesus were willing to bear the punishment of God's people, but only Jesus could be accepted by God because He Himself was without sin (Heb. 7:26–27).

12–16.   Both Moses and Jesus were dependent on personal communion with God. The results of this communion were manifested in various unique ways.

19.   The name of God reveals the nature of God. Through Moses, God revealed Himself as eternal* and unchanging; through Jesus, He revealed Himself as Father. (See Matthew 11:27; Romans 8:15.)

20.   The manna provided through Moses only sustained temporary, physical life. Some of those who ate it died later under God's judgment*. (See Numbers 14:22–23, 32; 26:63–65.) But through Jesus, the believer receives eternal* life. (See John 6:47–51.)

21–22.   The slavery from which Moses delivered Israel was physical; the slavery from which Jesus delivers the believer is spiritual.

25–26.   Israel broke the first covenant that God made with them, but God promised to make a new covenant that would provide forgiveness for all their sins (Jer. 31:31–34). Jesus came to institute this new covenant.

CONCLUSION:

This study brings out twenty-six points of clear resemblance between Moses and Jesus. It would be impossible to find any other prophet who has arisen in Israel, except Jesus, who resembles Moses in even a small number of these points. Therefore, it is unreasonable to deny that Jesus is the prophet whom Moses foretold in Deuteronomy 18:18–19.

However, if Jesus is the prophet whom Moses foretold, it is of the utmost importance for us to recognize this fact and act upon it. God said concerning this prophet, *"Whoever will not hear My words, which He speaks in My name, I will require it of him"* (Deut. 18:19).

The choice, then, is between the judgment* of God or His blessing: Judgment* if we reject Jesus, God's prophet; blessing if we acknowledge Him.

THIRD PROGRESS ASSESSMENT

CONGRATULATIONS...AGAIN!

You have now completed **sixteen studies**, with only one more section to complete. Consider for a moment what this means!

In the section you just finished, you made a detailed analysis of some of the most profound and important themes ever unfolded in the world's literature. These include:

- The history and destiny of Israel.

- The lives and characters of three of the greatest men who have ever crossed the stage of human history: Abraham, Moses, and Jesus.

- The central theme of all biblical prophecy: the life and work of the Messiah-Redeemer.

In so doing, you have searched out for yourself in the Bible the answers to nearly two hundred specific questions.

You have also committed to memory a total of twenty-three key verses of Scripture.

Take courage! There are only a few more lessons left to complete the course. Then you will find yourself more equipped to go on to enjoy the benefits of knowing God in this world.

Now, a word about what lies ahead. Studies 17, 18, and 19 will lead you on to the great climax of all history: the personal return of Jesus. Here you will find a number of signs you can look for that signal His return. Then you will answer the questions in the Final Review. Last of all, Study 20 brings all the strands together in a personal application. Press on! You're doing well!

THIRD REVIEW

Before you go on to the new material in the remaining studies, you will need to check yourself to see that you fully understand all the rich material contained in studies 12 through 16. The better you understand these, the better you will be able to grasp the exciting new material that lies ahead.

The method followed in this third review is the same as the others. First, read carefully through all the questions of the preceding five studies, together with the correct answers. Check that you know and understand the reason for each correct answer.

Second, review every Scripture passage from these eight studies that you learned for Memory Work.

Third, read carefully through the following questions and consider how you would answer them. Each question is related in some way to the material you have been studying.

1. What lessons from the history of Israel would you say are still applicable to Israel and to other nations today?

2. What acts of mercy was Jesus empowered to do by the anointing of the Holy Spirit upon Him?

3. State ten incidents in the life of Jesus that fulfilled specific prophecies of the Old Testament.

4. State ten important points of resemblance between Moses and Jesus.

Finally, write out on a separate sheet of paper your own answers to the above questions.

*   *   *   *   *

There are no marks allotted for this third review. Its purpose is to help you consolidate all that you have been discovering. When you are satisfied that this has been achieved, turn the page to Study 17.

PART FOUR

THE FUTURE

STUDY SEVENTEEN
THE SECOND COMING OF CHRIST

INTRODUCTION:

Jesus Christ first came to earth over two thousand years ago. The details of His coming were told in advance in sacred writings—prophecies—in the Bible. His first coming happened exactly as written in these prophecies.

When Jesus left this earth to return to heaven, He guaranteed His disciples that He would come back to the earth again. Besides Jesus' own promises, there are many more prophecies throughout the Bible about the second coming of Jesus, the Messiah. In fact, there are more prophecies in the Bible about His second coming than about His first coming.

Since the prophecies of His first coming happened exactly as written, it is sensible to believe that the prophecies of His second coming will be fulfilled in the same way.

The Scriptures in this study contain the clear promises of Christ's return. They also tell us what will happen to Christians at that time and how Christians must prepare themselves now.

MEMORY WORK: LUKE 21:36

❑ Check here after memorizing the verse. (Review verses from prior lessons daily.)

STUDY QUESTIONS

A. PROMISES OF CHRIST'S RETURN

1. For what purpose did Christ say He was leaving His disciples? (John 14:2)

_____

2. What promise did Christ give His disciples when He left them? (John 14:3)

_____

3. When Christ was taken to heaven, what promise did the angels give? (Acts 1:11)

_____

_____

4. What is the *"blessed hope"* to which all true Christians look forward? (Titus 2:13)

_____

5. What three sounds will be heard when Christ descends from heaven? (1 Thess. 4:16)

(1) _____   (2) _____

(3) _____

B. WHAT WILL HAPPEN TO CHRISTIANS

6. Will all Christians have died (sleep) when the Messiah comes? (1 Cor. 15:51)

_____

7. At this time, what will happen to Christians who have died? (1 Thess. 4:16)

_____

8. What two things will then happen to all Christians, whether they have died or not?

(1) (1 Cor. 15:51) _____

(2) (1 Thess. 4:17) _____

9. Will these Christians ever again be separated from the Lord? (1 Thess. 4:17)

_____

10. When we actually see the Lord, what change will take place in us? (1 John 3:2)

_____

11. As a result of this change, what will the body of the Christian then be like? (Phil. 3:21)

_____

12. What two words does Paul use to describe the body of the Christian after resurrection*? (1 Cor. 15:53)

   (1) _____   (2) _____

13. How does the Bible describe the feast that Christians will then enjoy? (Rev. 19:9)

_____

C. How Christians Must Prepare

14. What did the Lamb's bride do before the marriage supper? (Rev. 19:7)

_____

15.
What kind of clothing did she wear? (Rev. 19:8)

_____

16. What does the fine linen represent? (Rev. 19:8)

_____

17. Of the ten virgins, which ones went in to the marriage? (Matt. 25:10)

_____

18. If a man has the hope of seeing Jesus when He returns, how does he prepare himself for this? (1 John 3:3)

_____

19. To whom will Jesus appear the second time for salvation*? (Heb. 9:28)

_____

20. What two things must we do if we want to see the Lord? (Heb. 12:14)

(1) _____ (2) _____

21. What will be three marks of true Christians when Jesus returns? (2 Peter 3:14)

(1) _____ (2) _____

(3) _____

22. What words did Jesus use to show how sudden His coming will be? (Rev. 3:3; 16:15)

_____

23. Who knows the day and hour of Jesus' coming? (Mark 13:32)

_____

24. What did Christ Jesus warn all Christians to do in view of His coming? (Mark 13:35–37)

_____

25. What did Jesus warn Christians to do besides watching? (Luke 21:36)

_____

26. What three things did Jesus warn Christians could keep them from being ready? (Luke 21:34)

(1) _____ (2) _____

(3) _____

MEMORY WORK: LUKE 21:36

Write out this verse from memory.

_____

DO NOT TURN THIS PAGE UNTIL YOU HAVE COMPLETED ALL ANSWERS
IN THIS STUDY

CORRECT ANSWERS AND MARKS
STUDY SEVENTEEN

Question	Answers	Points
1.	To go and prepare a place for them	1
2.	That He would come again and receive them to Himself	2
3.	This same Jesus will come in like manner as you saw Him go into heaven	2
4.	The glorious appearing of our great God and Savior Jesus Christ	2
5.	(1) A shout	1
	(2) The voice of the archangel	1
	(3) The trumpet of God	1
6.	No	1
7.	They will rise (from the dead)	1
8.	(1) They will all be changed	1
	(2) They will all be caught up in the clouds to meet the Lord in the air	1
9.	No; never	1
10.	We will be like Him	1
11.	Like the glorious (glorified*) body of Christ	1
12.	(1) Incorruption*	1
	(2) Immortality*	1
13.	The marriage supper of the Lamb (Jesus)	1
14.	She made herself ready	1
15.	Fine linen, clean and bright (white)	1
16.	The righteous* acts of the saints	1
17.	Those who were ready	1
18.	He purifies himself just as He (Jesus) is pure	2
19.	To those who eagerly wait for Him	1
20.	(1) Pursue peace with all people	1
	(2) Pursue holiness	1

21.   (1) In peace   1
       (2) Without spot   1
       (3) Blameless   1

22.   As a thief   1

23.   No one knows, only God the Father   1

24.   To watch   1

25.   To pray always   1

26.   (1) Carousing (partying)   1
       (2) Drunkenness   1
       (3) Cares of this life   1

Check your memory card for written memory work.
If your memory work is word perfect, 4 points.   4
(1 point off for each mistake. If there are more than
3 mistakes, do not mark any points for the verse.)
                                                          _____
                                                 TOTAL   43

22 correct answers = 50%   30 correct answers = 70%   34 correct answers = 80%

NOTES ON CORRECT ANSWERS
STUDY SEVENTEEN

(The numbers on this page refer back to the numbers on the Correct Answers page.)

1–5.   *"By the mouth of two or three witnesses every word may be established"* (Matt. 18:16). Concerning the return of Christ we have the three witnesses: (1) Christ Himself (John 14:3); (2) the angels (Acts 1:11); (3) the apostle Paul (1 Thess. 4:16). Note the emphasis on the return of Christ in person: *"This same Jesus"* (Acts 1:11), *"The Lord Himself"* (1 Thess. 4:16). This *"blessed hope"* (Titus 2:13) is the highest goal of Christian living.

5.   (1) The shout will come from the Lord Himself. His voice alone has power to call forth the dead. (See John 5:28–29.) (2) The archangel will likely be Gabriel. His special duty is to proclaim when God is about to move in the affairs of men. (See Luke 1:19, 26.) (3) The trumpet is used to call God's people together. (See Numbers 10:2–3.)

6.   To *"sleep"* (1 Cor. 15:51) means to die. (Compare Acts 7:60 and 1 Corinthians 11:30.) This word is used for the death of Christians because they look forward to waking again on the resurrection* morning.

6–8.   The order of events is: (1) Dead (sleeping) Christians will be raised with new, glorified* bodies. (2) Living Christians will have their bodies changed in a flash to similar glorified* bodies. (3) All Christians will be caught up together in clouds to meet the Lord as He comes down from heaven.

10–12.   The glorified* body of the Christian will be like the Lord's own glorified* body. (For a fuller study of this subject, see my book *The Spirit-filled Believer's Handbook*, Part VI, Resurrection of the Dead.)

13.   Compare Matthew 8:11 and Matthew 26:29.

14–21,   The Bible very clearly teaches that, in order to be ready for the return of Christ,
24–25.   Christians must work hard to prepare themselves. In Revelation 19:8, the exact meaning of the *"fine linen"* is *"the righteous* acts of the saints."* This is the righteousness* of Christ, received by faith*, which is worked out in the day-to-day lives of Christians. (Compare Philippians 2:12–13: *"Work out...for it is God who works in you."*)

In this respect, God's Word directs Christians to prepare themselves by righteous* acts of:

1. Purity (being without spot) (1 John 3:3 and 2 Peter 3:14)

        2. Holiness (Heb. 12:14)

        3. Peace (right relations with all men) (Heb. 12:14 and 2 Peter 3:14)

        4. Blamelessness (being faithful in all Christian duties) (2 Peter 3:14)

        5. Hopefulness (waiting eagerly for Jesus) (Heb. 9:28)

        6. Watchfulness (Mark 13:37)

        7. Prayerfulness (Luke 21:36)

22.   Christ will be like a thief in the way He comes, but He will take only what is His own—*"those who are Christ's at His coming"* (1 Cor. 15:23).

23.   When the moment comes, the Father will tell the Son. Then all heaven will be stirred to action.

26.   (1) Jesus often warned against too much eating and drinking before He warned against drunkenness.

        (3) Compare Luke 17:27–28. The things mentioned here are not sinful in themselves. The sin comes from being too wrapped up in them.

STUDY EIGHTEEN
SIGNS OF CHRIST'S SECOND COMING

INTRODUCTION:

The Bible tells us of many special things that will happen in the world just before Christ's second coming. These things will be signs to warn us that He is coming soon.

In this study, some of the most important signs are stated. They are divided into two groups:

A. Signs in the World of Religion

B. Signs in the World at Large

Below each group of signs are given the references to the passages of Scripture in which those signs are mentioned. In this study, you are required to do the following:

1. Read through the signs in Group A.

2. Read through the Scriptures that are listed below Group A.

3. On the line below each sign, write in the reference of the Scripture that mentions it.

4. Repeat the same process for Group B.

5. At the end of each sign, you will see a square box. When you have done the rest of the study, read through the signs once again, and check each box if you feel that particular sign is being fulfilled in the world as you know it today.

(NOTE: There is one correct Scripture reference for each sign. However, in Group B, Matthew 24:7 applies to three different signs. Write in Matthew 24:7 after each sign to which it applies.)

MEMORY WORK: LUKE 21:28

❏ Check here after memorizing the verse. (Review verses from prior lessons daily.)

STUDY QUESTIONS

A. SIGNS IN THE WORLD OF RELIGION

1. Outpouring of the Holy Spirit across the world _____ ❏

2. Evangelism and missionary activity across the world _____ ❏

3. Christians put down, hated, tortured, and killed in all nations _____ ❏

4. Many false prophets _____ ❏

5. A great falling away from the Christian faith*

_____ ❏

6. Many Christians, misled by the Devil, giving in to deceiving spirits

_____ ❏

7. The love of many Christians growing cold _____ ❏

SCRIPTURE REFERENCES:

Matthew 24:12   1 Timothy 4:1   Matthew 24:9   Acts 2:17
Matthew 24:11   2 Thessalonians 2:3   Matthew 24:14

B. SIGNS IN THE WORLD AT LARGE

8. Great international wars; nation will rise against nation _____ ❏

9. Increase of travel and knowledge _____ ❏

10. Rise of Zionism* and rebuilding of Israel

_____ ❏

11. Jerusalem liberated from the rule of Gentiles* _____ ❏

12. Many scoffers denying the Word of God and the promise of Christ's return

_____ ❏

13. People locked in material pleasures and day-to-day living and forgetting the coming judgments* of God _____ ❏

14. Great decline in moral and upright living, along with the decline of outward forms of religion _____ ❏

15. Lawlessness will abound

_____ ❏

16. Famines and pestilences _____ ❏

17. Earthquakes in many places _____ ❏

18. Distress of nations and perplexity (confusion) _____ ❏ ❏

19. Many antichrists _____ ❏ ❏

SCRIPTURE REFERENCES:

Matthew 24:12	Luke 21:24	1 John 2:18	2 Peter 3:2–7
Daniel 12:4	Matthew 24:7	Luke 17:26–30	Psalm 102:16
	2 Timothy 3:1–5	Luke 21:25	

MEMORY WORK: LUKE 21:28

Write out this verse from memory.

DO NOT TURN THIS PAGE UNTIL YOU HAVE COMPLETED ALL ANSWERS IN THIS STUDY

CORRECT ANSWERS AND MARKS
STUDY EIGHTEEN

Question	Answers	Points
1.	Acts 2:17	1
2.	Matthew 24:14	1
3.	Matthew 24:9	1
4.	Matthew 24:11	1
5.	2 Thessalonians 2:3	1
6.	1 Timothy 4:1	1
7.	Matthew 24:12	1
8.	Matthew 24:7	1
9.	Daniel 12:4	1
10.	Psalm 102:16	1
11.	Luke 21:24	1
12.	2 Peter 3:2–7	1
13.	Luke 17:26–30	1
14.	2 Timothy 3:1–5	1
15.	Matthew 24:12	1
16.	Matthew 24:7	1
17.	Matthew 24:7	1
18.	Luke 21:25	1
19.	1 John 2:18	1

Check your memory card for written memory work.
If your memory work is word perfect, 4 points.   4
(1 point off for each mistake. If there are more than
3 mistakes, do not mark any points for the verse.)

                                                    TOTAL   23

12 correct answers = 50%   16 correct answers = 70%   18 correct answers = 80%

THREE FINAL IMPORTANT QUESTIONS:

There are nineteen different signs of Christ's coming mentioned in this study.

1. Next to how many of them did you place a check?
2. Does this indicate to you that Christ may be coming soon?
3. If so, are you ready?

NOTES ON CORRECT ANSWERS
STUDY EIGHTEEN

(The numbers on this page refer back to the numbers on the Correct Answers page.)

1. The expression *"all flesh"* means the entire human race. It is often used with this meaning in the Prophets (Isa. 40:5–6) (Jer. 25:31) (Ezek. 21:4–5). Every part of the human race will feel the impact of this last great outpouring of God's Spirit.

2. Bringing the gospel to other people and nations is the natural effect of the outpouring of God's Spirit. Note the special comment after this sign: *"And then the end will come"* (Matt. 24:14).

3. There were more Christian martyrs* in the twentieth century than in any other century. For example, many communist countries persecute Christians as a matter of state policy.

4–6. These three signs all point to a great increase in satanic pressures and deceptions aimed at luring Christians from their loyalty to Christ. The Bible indicates that, at the end, there will be only two main groups of Christians. One is described as a "bride" and the other as a "harlot." The bride is faithful to the Bridegroom (Christ). The harlot is unfaithful to Christ. (See Revelation 17–18.)

7. This sign matches the picture of the church in Laodicea. The damning sin of these Christians is being *"lukewarm"*; they are neither hot nor cold (Rev. 3:14–22). This decline in the love by Christians will be mainly due to one or more of the following factors: (1) Christians being bitterly persecuted; (2) Christians being tricked by the Devil; (3) Christians living mainly for money and material comfort.

8. The last century has seen wars greater and more numerous than any other century, especially the two world wars.

9. Note how these two factors are logically connected. The increase in knowledge (science) makes possible the increase in travel. Likewise, more travel increases knowledge.

10–11. The rise of Zionism*, the rebirth of the state of Israel, and the Six-Day War of 1967 are among the great miracles of modern history. Someone has said, "The Jews are the minute hand on God's prophetic clock, and that hand has almost reached midnight."

12. The last century has seen repeated bold attacks on the Bible unlike any other century. It is ironic that these attacks on the Bible actually confirm its accuracy since the Bible clearly predicts them.

13–15, 18.	These signs are proved to be true daily by the newspapers of the modern world. (Compare Luke 17:26 with Genesis 6:5, 12–13.) The three main evil features of Noah's day were: (1) evil thoughts and desires; (2) degraded and immoral sex; (3) violence.
16.	Famines and plagues naturally tend to go together, and both are often caused by war.
17.	Records over the past century show a striking increase in the number of earthquakes.
19.	The work of *"the spirit of the antichrist"* (1 John 4:3) is twofold: first, to move Christ from His supreme, God-given position of authority; second, to raise up someone else in Christ's place. In this sense, the main political ideologies of this and past generations—Islam, Fascism, and Communism—have all been anti-Christian (as are many other political and religious forces at work in the world today). However, the world still awaits the final Antichrist, as described in 2 Thessalonians 2:3–12.

STUDY NINETEEN
CHRIST'S KINGDOM ESTABLISHED ON EARTH

INTRODUCTION:

Christ's kingdom on earth will be ushered in by His judgments* on all who have rejected God's mercy and opposed God's purposes in the preceding period. On the other hand, all believers who have been either resurrected* or supernaturally changed at His coming will be allotted various positions of authority in His kingdom. With Jerusalem as His capital, Jesus will reign over all nations for one thousand years, bringing justice, peace, prosperity, and the knowledge of God to the whole earth. Finally, He will offer up Himself and His kingdom in submission to God the Father.

MEMORY WORK: 2 TIMOTHY 2:11–12

❑ Check here after memorizing the verse. (Review verses from prior lessons daily.)

STUDY QUESTIONS

A. JUDGMENTS* THAT USHER IN MESSIAH'S KINGDOM

1. The coming of Jesus from heaven is described in 2 Thessalonians 1:6–10.

    (1) How will He deal with the wicked and disobedient? (v. 8)

    _____

    (2) What will be their punishment? (v. 9)

    _____

    _____

2. What will happen to the Beast (Antichrist) and the False Prophet? (Rev. 19:20)

    _____

    _____

3. How will Jesus rule the nations on earth? (Rev. 19:11–15) (Ps. 2:7–9)

    _____

4. When Jesus sets up His throne on earth, who will be gathered before Him for judgment*? (Matt. 25:31–32) (Joel 3:1–2)

    _____

5. These nations will be judged by the way they have treated a certain class of people. How does Jesus describe this class?

    (1) (Matt. 25:40) _____

    (2) (Joel 3:2) _____

6. What will be the double reward of those nations who have done what Jesus required?

    (1) (Matt. 25:34) _____

    (2) (Matt. 25:46) _____

7. What will be the punishment of those nations who have not done what Jesus required? (Matt. 25:41, 46)

    _____

    _____

B. The Position of Resurrected* Believers

8. If we endure suffering for Jesus, what two rewards can we expect?

    (1) (Rom. 8:17) _____

    (2) (2 Tim. 2:12) _____

9. What position did Jesus promise to the apostles who had continued faithfully with Him? (Matt. 19:27–28)

    _____

10. To what kind of believer will Jesus give authority to rule the nations with Him? (Rev. 2:26–27)

_____

11. What will be the double reward of those believers beheaded by the Antichrist for their witness to Jesus? (Rev. 20:4–5)

(1) _____

(2) _____

12. Jesus told a parable about servants administering money committed to them by their master. (See Luke 19:12–27.) What was the reward:

(1) Of the servant who achieved a tenfold increase? (Luke 19:16–17)

_____

(2) Of the servant who achieved a fivefold increase? (Luke 19:18–19)

_____

13. Name two areas over which resurrected* believers will rule as judges in the next age?

(1) (1 Cor. 6:2) _____

(2) (1 Cor. 6:3) _____

C. A Prophetic Preview of Messiah's Kingdom

14. With what kind of scepter does Christ rule? (Ps. 45:6) (Heb. 1:8)

_____

15. Why has God anointed Jesus above all others? (Ps. 45:7) (Heb. 1:9)

_____

16. In what place has the Lord chosen to dwell forever? (Ps. 132:13–14)

_____

17. What names are given to the place where the Lord will reign as king? (Isa. 24:23)

    (1) (Ps. 48:1–2) _____

    (2) (Matt. 5:34–35) _____

18. In the latter days, what mountain will be raised above the surrounding mountains? (Isa. 2:2) (Mic. 4:1)

    _____

19. Who will flow to this mountain? (Isa. 2:2) (Mic. 4:1)

    _____

20. What will God teach these nations? (Isa. 2:3) (Mic. 4:2)

    _____

21. What two things will go forth out of Zion and Jerusalem? (Isa. 2:3) (Mic. 4:2)

    (1) _____ (2) _____

22. When Messiah judges the nations, what two things will they no longer do? (Isa. 2:4) (Mic. 4:3)

    (1) _____

    (2) _____

23. For what special feast will nations go up to Jerusalem each year? (Zech. 14:16)

    _____

24. Psalm 72 foreshows various features of the reign of David's Son, the Messiah. For example:

(1) How will He rule the poor? (verses 2, 4) _____

(2) What three kinds of people will Messiah deliver*? (verse 12)

    (a) _____ (b) _____

    (c) _____

(3) What kind of person will flourish during Messiah's reign? (v. 7)

_____

(4) Of what will there be abundance? (v. 7)

_____

(5) What two things will all nations do for Messiah?

    (a) (v. 11) _____

    (b) (v. 17) _____

25. What will be three permanent results of Messiah's righteous* rule? (Isa. 32:17)

    (1) _____   (2) _____

    (3) _____

26. For how long will this period of Christ's reign last? (Rev. 20:4, 5)

_____

27. What will Christ do at the end of this period? (1 Cor. 15:24, 28)

_____

28. What is the end purpose of God in all this? (1 Cor. 15:28)

_____

MEMORY WORK: 2 TIMOTHY 2:11–12

Write out these verses from memory.

_____

DO NOT TURN THIS PAGE UNTIL YOU HAVE COMPLETED ALL ANSWERS IN THIS STUDY

CORRECT ANSWERS AND MARKS
STUDY NINETEEN

Question	Answers	Points
1.	(1) He will take vengeance on them with flaming fire	1
	(2) Everlasting destruction from the presence of the Lord and from the glory of His power	2
2.	They will be cast alive into the lake of fire burning with brimstone	1
3.	With a rod of iron	1
4.	All nations	1
5.	(1) My brethren	1
	(2) My people, My heritage Israel	2
6.	(1) They will inherit Christ's kingdom	1
	(2) They will receive eternal* life	1
7.	Everlasting punishment in everlasting fire prepared for the Devil and his angels	2
8.	(1) We will be glorified* together with Him	1
	(2) We will reign with Him	1
9.	To sit on twelve thrones judging the twelve tribes of Israel	2
10.	The one who overcomes and keeps Christ's works until the end	2
11.	(1) To reign with Christ for one thousand years	1
	(2) To have part in the first resurrection*	1
12.	(1) Authority over ten cities	1
	(2) Authority over five cities	1
13.	(1) The world	1
	(2) Angels	1
14.	A scepter of righteousness*	1
15.	Because He loves righteousness* and hates wickedness (lawlessness)	2
16.	Zion	1
17.	(1) Mount Zion	1
	(2) Jerusalem	1
18.	The mountain of the Lord's house	1

19.	All nations (peoples)	1
20.	His ways	1
21.	(1) The law	1
	(2) The Word of the Lord	1
22.	(1) Lift up their swords against other nations	1
	(2) Learn war anymore	1
23.	The Feast of Tabernacles	1
24.	(1) With justice	1
	(2) (a) The needy	1
	(b) The poor	1
	(c) The one who has no helper	1
	(3) The righteous*	1
	(4) Peace	1
	(5) (a) Serve Him	1
	(b) Call Him blessed	1
25.	(1) Peace	1
	(2) Quietness	1
	(3) Assurance	1
26.	A thousand years	1
27.	Deliver the kingdom to God the Father and be subject to Him	2
28.	That God may be all in all	1

Check your memory card for written memory work.
If your memory work is word perfect, 4 points for each verse. 8
(1 point off for each mistake in a verse. If there are more than
3 mistakes, do not mark any points for that verse.)

TOTAL   62

31 correct answers = 50%   43 correct answers = 70%   50 correct answers = 80%

NOTES ON CORRECT ANSWERS
STUDY NINETEEN

(The numbers on this page refer back to the numbers on the Correct Answers page.)

1. Second Thessalonians 1:6–10 depicts the glory and power of Christ's coming. All His enemies will be eternally* banished, but His glory will be seen both in the angels who accompany Him and in the believers who will be caught up to meet Him. (Compare 1 Thessalonians 4:16–17.)

2. Revelation 13 reveals that, as this age draws to a close, human wickedness will come to a head in the person of a supremely wicked, but powerful, ruler described as *"the beast"* (Rev. 7:11). He is also called *"the man of sin* [lawlessness]" (2 Thess. 2:3), *"the son of perdition"* (v. 3), and *"the Antichrist"* (1 John 2:18). He will be supported by an evil religious leader called *"the false prophet"* (Rev. 16:13). Together, they will seek to destroy all the followers of Jesus. (Compare Daniel 8:23–25.)

3. Revelation 19:11–15 depicts the coming of Jesus as King and Judge, with supreme power and authority to deal with all wickedness.

4–7. The judgment* of the nations here described will determine which nations will be admitted to the Lord's kingdom and which will be excluded from it. The basis of their judgment* will be the way they have treated the brothers of Jesus, the Jewish people. Jesus reckons anything done to the Jews—either good or bad—as done to Himself.

8–13. When Jesus returns and sets up His kingdom, all believers who have served Him faithfully in this life will be exalted to positions of honor and authority. They will share with Jesus in the government of the universe. (Compare Revelation 3:21.) The degree of honor and authority assigned to believers will correspond to their faithfulness in serving Jesus in this age.

14–15. The distinctive feature of Christ's character will be reflected in His kingdom: righteousness*. Without righteousness*, there can never be true or lasting peace. (Compare Romans 14:17.)

16–17. The Lord's kingdom will have its earthly capital in Jerusalem, or Zion. This is an important reason to pray for the peace of Jerusalem. (See Psalm 122:6.) The rest of the earth will never know true peace until Jerusalem is established in peace.

18. At present, Mount Zion is lower than the mountains around it, but at the Lord's coming, tremendous geologic changes will elevate Mount Zion above these surrounding mountains. (Compare Zechariah 14:3–11.)

19–23.   Jerusalem will then be the world center for worship, for government, and for instruction in the ways of God. This will bring about worldwide disarmament and lasting peace.

24–25.   The following are main features of Christ's reign: righteousness*; justice (especially for the underprivileged); peace; prosperity; universal acknowledgment of Christ as God's appointed ruler. The establishment of His kingdom is the only realistic solution to the problems of disease, famine, injustice, and war.

26.   The precise duration of Christ's reign is stated six times in Revelation 20—in verses 2, 3, 4, 5, 6, and 7.

27–28.   The delivering up of the kingdom to God the Father fulfills the principle stated in Romans 11:36. All things have their source in God the Father, and all things find their fulfillment in Him. However, the Father relates to the universe through His Son, the Messiah.

FINAL PROGRESS ASSESSMENT

Your faith* and perseverance have been rewarded! You have now completed all the main nineteen studies. The only one remaining is an exercise in personal application.

It is time to pause and look back to see how far you have come.

You have seen how God's Word and God's Spirit, working together, can equip you with all you need for a life of fruitfulness and victory in His service.

In Study 4, you learned the importance and significance of water baptism. Then, in Studies 10 and 11, you learned about your responsibility to take your place in the long and honorable line of God's witnesses through the centuries; and also about the abundant provision that God has made for your material needs.

You saw how Messiah's atonement provided the divine remedy for the two basic problems of the human race: sin and sickness. You have learned how to apply this remedy in your own life and in the lives of others.

You have traced the master plan of history from its modest beginning in Abraham through the prophets and statesmen of Israel to the manifestation of the promised Messiah-Redeemer.

Finally, you have had a brief but exciting preview of the event with which this age will close: the personal return of Jesus in power and glory to establish His kingdom on earth.

In doing all this, you have searched out for yourself in the Bible the answers to over 650 specific questions. You have also committed to memory twenty-seven key verses of Scripture.

The challenge of Study 20 now awaits you. But before moving on to that, be sure to work carefully through the Final Review on the next page.

FINAL REVIEW

Before you go on to Study 20, it is important for you to make sure that you have fully mastered all the material contained in studies 17 through 19. This will help you to prepare for the final personal application.

The method followed in the final review is similar to that followed in the first two.

First, read carefully through all the questions of the preceding three studies, together with the corresponding correct answers. Check that you now know and understand the correct answer to each question.

Second, review all the Scripture verses in these three studies that you have learned for Memory Work.

Third, read carefully through the following questions and consider how you would answer them. Each question is related in some way to the material you have been studying.

1. What are the main things that you should do to prepare yourself for Christ's return?

2. List ten signs in the world that indicate Christ is coming soon.

3. What does the bride's *"fine linen, clean and bright"* (Rev. 19:8) refer to? Is your garment ready?

4. In what ways will you be changed at the resurrection?

Finally, write out on a separate sheet of paper your own answers to the above questions.

* * * * *

There are no marks allotted for this final review. Its purpose is to help you consolidate all that you have been discovering. When you are satisfied that this has been achieved, turn the page to Study 20: Personal Application.

STUDY TWENTY
REVIEW AND PERSONAL APPLICATION

INTRODUCTION:

The purpose of this last study is to fix firmly in your mind the many important truths that you have learned.

Review is a key part of all learning that lasts. By working step-by-step through this last study, you will greatly add to the benefit and blessing that you have received from this course. Also, you will find out for yourself just how much you have really learned. Do not forget to do the review of the memory work!

FINAL MEMORY WORK: JAMES 1:25

❏ Check here after memorizing the verse. (Review verses from prior lessons daily.)

First, read through all the questions of the other nineteen studies, together with the correct answers. Be sure that you know and understand the correct answer to each question.

Second, review all the Bible verses that you have learned for Memory Work.

Third, write the answers to Sections A and B below.

STUDY QUESTIONS

SECTION A:

In the spaces provided below, write four important truths from the Bible that you have learned from this course. In each case, include the references to the verses in the Bible where that truth is found.

First truth

_____

_____

_____

Bible references

Second truth

_____

_____

_____

    Bible references

Third truth

_____

_____

_____

    Bible references

Fourth truth

_____

_____

_____

    Bible references

SECTION B:

In the space below, describe briefly any important changes that have taken place in your own life because of this study of the Bible.

_____

_____

_____

_____

_____

_____

NOTE: There are no points given for Sections A and B above.

FINAL MEMORY WORK: JAMES 1:25

Write out this verse from memory.

Correct Answers and marks

STUDY TWENTY

Check your memory card for written memory work.
If your memory work is word perfect, 4 points.   4
(1 point off for each mistake. If there are more than
3 mistakes, do not mark any points for the verse.)

TOTAL   4

MARKS FOR THE COURSE

Write your points for each study in the space provided below in the right-hand column. Add up your own total and compare it with the standards given for Pass, Very Good, or Excellent.

Study No. 1	49	_____
Study No. 2	54	_____
Study No. 3	38	_____
Study No. 4	36	_____
Study No. 5	38	_____
Study No. 6	59	_____
Study No. 7	49	_____
Study No. 8	40	_____
Study No. 9	44	_____
Study No. 10	44	_____
Study No. 11	47	_____
Study No. 12	54	_____
Study No. 13	48	_____
Study No. 14	51	_____
Study No. 15	61	_____
Study No. 16	33	_____
Study No. 17	43	_____
Study No. 18	23	_____
Study No. 19	62	_____
Study No. 20	4	_____
Total	877	TOTAL_____

PASS = 50% and over (439)

VERY GOOD = 70% and over (614)

EXCELLENT = 80% and over (702)

*   *   *   *   *

Congratulations on completing the course!

Now you will want to continue exploring the truths of the Bible through further systematic study.

After the Glossary pages, you will find a list of other helpful Bible teaching materials, which will lead you into a fuller understanding of God's plan and provision for you as a Christian.

*   *   *   *   *

GLOSSARY

Adamic — coming from Adam, the first created man

ascension — going upward, especially Jesus rising to heaven from the earth

blasphemy — slander; abusive words

confess, confessed, confession — to speak out in public

deliver, deliverance — to set free, as from misery or evil

eternal, eternity, eternally — time that lasts forever

faith — a conviction, trust, belief or assurance

Gentiles — heathen nations, especially people who are not Jewish

glorify, glorifying, glorified — to take on an aspect of God's greatness

hallowed — used to describe something that is holy

immortality — the state of living forever, not subject to death

incorruptible, incorruption — not able to be destroyed or spoiled

judgment — making a decision that determines one's guilt

justification — to be free from a charge or accusation, declared righteous

martyrs — those who died for their faith

meditate, meditation — to think often or deeply about something

oppress, oppressed — to treat people cruelly so that they don't have the same freedom or benefits as others

prophesy, prophesied, prophesying — to speak forth, bring a word directly from the Lord, often about the future

recompense — something received as a payment or reward, to make compensation

redemption	being set free because someone paid a ransom, being delivered from evil and the penalty of sin
remission (of sins)	a cancellation of all judgment or obligation
repent, repentance	a turning around; a change of mind and heart accompanied by a change of behavior
resurrection, resurrected	a restoration to life; rising from the dead
righteous, righteousness	the quality of being right because of the grace of God
salvation	rescue, deliverance; in Scripture it includes forgiveness, healing, prosperity, deliverance, safety, rescue, liberation, and restoration
sanctify, sanctification	to set apart, dedicate, consecrate, make or become holy
testimony	proof, evidence, or what someone can say from their personal experience to support what they believe to be true
transgression, transgressors	the breaking of a moral law or rule of behavior
Zionism	a movement that is focused on supporting the well-being of Israel

ABOUT THE AUTHOR

Derek Prince (1915–2003) was born in India of British parents. Educated as a scholar of Greek and Latin at Eton College and Cambridge University, England, he held a fellowship in ancient and modern philosophy at King's College. He also studied several modern languages, including Hebrew and Aramaic, at Cambridge University and the Hebrew University in Jerusalem.

While serving with the British army in World War II, he began to study the Bible and experienced a life-changing encounter with Jesus Christ. Out of this encounter he formed two conclusions: first, that Jesus Christ is alive; second, that the Bible is a true, relevant, up-to-date book. These conclusions altered the whole course of his life, which he then devoted to studying and teaching the Bible.

Derek's main gift of explaining the Bible and its teaching in a clear and simple way has helped build a foundation of faith in millions of lives. He wrote over fifty books, which have been translated in over sixty languages and distributed worldwide. His book *Shaping History through Prayer and Fasting* has awakened Christians around the world to their responsibility to pray for their governments. Many consider underground translations of the book as instrumental in the fall of communist regimes in the former USSR, East Germany, and Czechoslovakia. He pioneered teaching on such groundbreaking themes as generational curses, the biblical significance of Israel, and demonology. His radio program, now known as *Derek Prince Legacy Radio*, began in 1979 and has been translated into over a dozen languages. Estimates are that Derek Prince's clear, expositional teaching of the Bible has reached more than half the globe. His nondenominational, nonsectarian approach has made his teaching equally relevant and helpful to people from all racial and religious backgrounds.

Until a few years before his death in 2003 at the age of eighty-eight, Prince persisted in the ministry God had called him to as he traveled the world, imparting God's revealed truth, praying for the sick and afflicted, and sharing his prophetic insights into world events in the light of Scripture.

Internationally recognized as a Bible scholar and spiritual patriarch, Derek Prince established a teaching ministry that spanned six continents and more than sixty years. In 2002, he said, "It is my desire—and I believe the Lord's desire—that this ministry continue the work, which God began through me over sixty years ago, until Jesus returns."

With its international headquarters in Charlotte, North Carolina, Derek Prince Ministries continues to reach out to believers in over 140 countries with Derek's teaching, fulfilling the mandate to keep on "until Jesus returns." This is accomplished through the outreaches of more than thirty Derek Prince Ministries International offices around the world, including primary work in Australia, Canada, China, France, Germany, the Netherlands, New Zealand, Norway, Russia, South Africa, Switzerland, the United Kingdom, and the United States. For current information about these and other worldwide locations, visit www.derekprince.org.